A Man for All Seasons

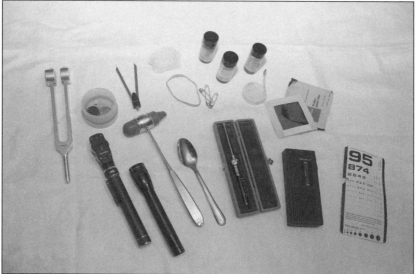

Top: Dr. Joynt's medical bag—small but powerful—was the ultimate in low-tech aid. *Bottom:* The bag's contents were the tools used by the master diagnostician. Photographs by Karen Harris.

A Man for All Seasons

Robert J. Joynt, MD, PhD

Nancy W. Bolger

MELIORA PRESS
An imprint of the University of Rochester Press

First published 2016

Meliora Press is an imprint of the
University of Rochester Press
668 Mt. Hope Avenue, Rochester, NY 14620, USA
www.urpress.com
and Boydell & Brewer Limited
PO Box 9, Woodbridge, Suffolk IP12 3DF, UK
www.boydellandbrewer.com

ISBN-13: 978-1-58046-570-0

Library of Congress Cataloging-in-Publication Data

Names: Bolger, Nancy W., author.
Title: A man for all seasons : Robert J. Joynt, MD, PHD / Nancy W.
    Bolger.
Description: Rochester, NY : Meliora Press, an imprint of the Univer-
    sity of Rochester Press, 2016. | Includes bibliographical references.
Identifiers: LCCN 2016022386 | ISBN 9781580465700 (hardcover :
    alk. paper)
Subjects: LCSH: Joynt, Robert J., 1925—Health. | Neurologists—
    United States—Biography. | Academic medical centers—New York
    (State)—Rochester—History—20th century.
Classification: LCC RC339.5 .B65 2016 | DDC 616.80092 [B]–dc23 LC
    record available at https://lccn.loc.gov/2016022386

This publication is printed on acid-free paper.
Printed in the United States of America.

*To Margaret McGivern Joynt,
and to the late Jules Cohen, MD, who had intended to tell this story.*

CONTENTS

Foreword by Robert Holloway ix

Preface xi

Acknowledgments xiii

1 Growing Up in Corn Country 1
2 Sergeant Joynt in India 8
3 Becoming "Dr. Bob" 12
4 Unraveling Neurology's Gordian Knot:
  Montreal, Canada 17
5 Unraveling Neurology's Gordian Knot:
  Cambridge, England 23
6 Unraveling Neurology's Gordian Knot:
  University of Iowa 31
7 Dr. Bob Builds a New Department 39
8 The Comic Spirit (and How He Wielded It) 50
9 Dean Bob's Ten Commandments for Interns 56
10 Dr. Bob, Editor Extraordinaire 59
11 Onward and Upward, Dr. Bob! 1966–84 66
12 "Low Intellect in High Places" 69
13 Stalking Sherlock Holmes 74
14 Dean Joynt Takes the Helm 80
15 Vice President Joynt's Team Builds for the Future 87
16 Dr. Bob's "Dark Days" 93
17 Life with Father 96
18 The Man of Faith 105

Appendix: Curriculum Vitae 109

Notes 127

Photographs follow page 68.

FOREWORD

"Where is that coming from? It's beautiful," said Christy Miller, administrator of the Department of Neurology, as she looked at a reflection of prism colors in my office on a rare sunny Rochester day in early December 2015. The source of the colors was an etched glass plaque on the windowsill entitled "2013 Dr. Robert Joynt Kindness Award." And each day when the sun shines, a brilliant rainbow of colors radiates against my office wall, refracted through the words "You can't always be right, but you can always be kind."

The rainbow symbolizes many things—life, hope, promise, divinity, creation, potential, harmony, spirituality, connection, transformation—and acts as a bridge between the earth and the sky. Nancy Bolger, in *A Man for All Seasons*, presents a portrait of a man who shined like a rainbow. Her style is as informal and informative and as modest and humorous as Bob Joynt himself. In eighteen short essays, she brings together the many lively colors of his life, rarely appreciated by those of us fortunate enough to see only one or two on the spectrum. As a result, we are able to see a near-perfect harmony of human qualities rarely glimpsed in any one individual. For this, we owe her a debt of gratitude.

Superheroes are two dimensional and larger than life. Real-life heroes are complex and diminutive. Bob had a rare combination of great intellect, common sense, wit, and charm. He had an uncanny ability to take people as they are and meet them on their own ground. He had a consistency and solidity of character, imbued with honesty and humility. He made us laugh and taught us how not to take ourselves too seriously. When needed, he was brave and courageous. We learned by watching his small acts of kindness, consideration, and care. And he knew he was a small part of something bigger than himself, contributing to work that would last much longer than any one lifetime.

Bob's life reinforces to all of us that the most important things we do in our lives, we do for others. It is what draws many of us to the medical profession in the first place. There is a thirst to learn, to care, to heal, and to pass on the knowledge we have gained to others. Those who give us the foundation on which to build our knowledge not only change our lives but they touch the lives of everyone else we teach in turn. Bob Joynt gave the gift of his life and knowledge to all of us. He made us feel safe while we watched and marveled how he taught us all with a disarming wit and twinkle in his eye. We must pass it forward to generations to come.

Just saying the name "Bob Joynt" brings a warm smile to the faces of those who knew him—whether one knew him as a husband, father, family man, friend, patient, neurologist, editor, sailor, scientist, medical student, resident, man of faith, chairman, dean, or vice president. While we all may have known Bob for different reasons and under different circumstances, we smile, and smile more. It is only fitting that we honor him on the fiftieth anniversary of the department he founded.

Bob Joynt was a real-life hero. He simply made us comfortable and made us feel better about the world around us, leaving it a much better place than how he found it. The following pages will tell you how.

Robert Holloway, MD, MPH
Professor and Chair, Department of Neurology
University of Rochester
Rochester, New York
February 28, 2016

PREFACE

One wintry afternoon in January 2015, Margaret Joynt and I were
enjoying tea by the fireside in my old house in Pittsford. Margaret had come to talk about a project. Did I know that Neurology,
the department at the University of Rochester Medical Center that
her husband, Bob, had founded and raised to international renown,
was having a fiftieth anniversary celebration in 2016? Yes, I did—and
wasn't that something to look forward to! Then Margaret shocked
me: "Nancy, I'd like you to write a remembrance of Bob for the occasion. You know, the years of his career really cover a big part of the
Medical Center's history." Carefully, a bit shakily, I put down my teacup. "Margaret, I'm honored—but no. For that, you need someone
like Oliver Sacks."

It was hard to say no to Margaret. My late husband, Stuart, and
I were friends of the Joynts, both outside the Medical Center and
within, where for several years I was a writer and editor. Though we
never worked closely together, Bob had asked me to help him and
Dr. Jules Cohen with the institution's seventy-fifth anniversary history in 2000. His inimitable note when I received a coveted honor
for medical research writing from the Association of American
Medical Colleges is a treasure. . . . Can you see where this is going?

Several days later, I was in the office of the neurology chair Dr.
Robert Holloway, talking about the Joynt project. I explained that
I couldn't write a conventional biography of Bob, nor was I able to
tell the full history of the Department of Neurology, an important
and complex organization with many moving parts. I *could* try to
capture the man and his life in a series of short, informal essays.
(I would be helped immeasurably, as it turned out, by interviews
recorded shortly after Dr. Joynt's death by his friends and faculty
colleagues Dr. Jules Cohen and Dr. Ruth Lawrence.) I have been
able to add Dr. Joynt's own voice to these pages by including autobiographical stories from his "Changes + People + Comments" section of *Neurology*, which ran monthly from 1998 to 2012.

The big question I had to answer that day was this: What identifier could I use in talking about this man of international renown who was more familiarly seen in Rochester as an informal, "down home" kind of guy, full of wit and good humor, and modest to a fault? To refer to him repeatedly as "Dr. Joynt" might hide the man behind the title. Still, that white coat and all it represents could not be ignored. "How about 'Dr. Bob'?" a neurologist friend suggested. That sounded right, and so it is as "Dr. Bob" that the remarkable Robert Joynt, MD, PhD, appears in these pages.

Nancy W. Bolger
Pittsford, New York
February 9, 2016

ACKNOWLEDGMENTS

Dozens of Dr. Robert Joynt's colleagues, friends, and family have helped write his story. Their names and their remembrances—some serious, some amusing—appear throughout these pages. They are the heart of this little book.

From the initial days of "the Joynt project" and throughout the following months, the child neurologist Dr. Gary Myers and his wife, Ruth, have embodied the word "friendship" through their encouragement and wise counsel.

Although grateful to all, I am especially indebted to the following persons: Robert Holloway, MD, chair of the Department of Neurology; Marshall Lichtman, MD, former dean of the University of Rochester School of Medicine; Paul Griner, MD, former CEO of Strong Memorial Hospital; G. Dennis O'Brien, PhD, former president of the University of Rochester; Christopher Hoolihan, head of the Miner Medical Library; Nancy Baldwin, Dr. Joynt's longtime assistant; and especially Margaret Joynt and the Joynt offspring, "six sired and five acquired."

1

GROWING UP IN CORN COUNTRY

"We tried to spoil Bobby, but he was unspoilable."
—Patty Joynt Olson, sister

It is three days before Christmas, 1925. Inside a room at Sacred Heart Hospital, a mother has just delivered a baby boy, her fourth child after three girls. Still wrapped in a cloud of anesthesia, she slowly opens her eyes—and ears—to an advent of young angels in her room, sweetly singing Christmas hymns. For a few moments, the devout mother is puzzled: "Am I in heaven?" Reality comes slowly: her "angels" are little schoolgirls from the convent across the street. And now, suddenly, she remembers her own Christmas miracle. Finally, the Joynt family has a baby boy.

The baby will grow up in this little town of Le Mars, Iowa, as the family's favorite possession—adored by his mother, pampered by his three sisters,[1] and cherished by his father. So much love was showered on little Bobby Joynt that he would later joke, "I was born at Christmas time—in a manger."

      ❧   ❧   ❧

Life was comfortable for the family of Dr. Robert J. Joynt, Sr., one of the town's dentists. Le Mars,[2] northeast of Sioux City, had a population of less than five thousand when our Dr. Bob was a kid. Surrounded by farms, this primarily agricultural community would later boast a major meat-packing industry and the biggest maker of ice-cream novelties in the country. In spite of the Great Depression, many of Le Mars's residents in 1930 saw the town for what it was—a Norman Rockwell kind of town, just right for families. A river ran through it, and the town park boasted a pavilion for band concerts;

there was a natural swimming pool with diving boards that was free and open, and a golf course that offered adults and teenagers both pleasure and plenty of the inevitable golfers' frustration. Schools were good. (Not until three years later would the town suddenly explode in angry labor strife.)

The Joynt family house, half a block from the county courthouse, was spacious and comfortable, with three bedrooms and a "sleeping porch" for the four children. (During the Midwest's violent summer thunderstorms, mother Mayme would protect her sleeping brood by sprinkling them with holy water.) A grassy front yard was fine for outdoor romping, the children vied with one another during games of pitch-and-catch and hide-and-seek, and sister Patty wrote plays staged in the neighbor's barn. A fireplace made winter evenings cozy, and in the evenings the youngsters sat on the rug playing games and listening to the radio with their parents.

The highlight of the summer was the month-long vacation at Lake Okoboji. "Our mother would drive the hundred-mile trip to Smiths' Cottages, which took about four hours," recalled Patty. Bobolink was a real camp with outdoor plumbing. For young Bobby, summer was heaven—and heaven on earth for him meant going barefoot. "As a kid," he would say later, "I always knew where my shoes were. I took them off after picking up my final report card, put them in the back seat of the car, our Hudson Essex, wore them for church on Sunday—and didn't put them back on for good until the first day of school."

Life may have been comfortable for the Joynts, but for them, and for most Americans during those Great Depression years, "Be thrifty!" was the daily rule. Farm families who could afford to go to "Doc" Joynt's dental office often paid their bills with a chicken or a bag of vegetables. Mother Mayme made—and remade—her daughter's dresses; the family's one bicycle (a boy's model!) was shared by all four children. When fifteen-year-old Bob wanted a drum, his adoring mother provided it—by selling her engagement ring.

Still, the Joynts always had enough to share. These were days when men without jobs—the hoboes—rode the rails across country looking for work and food. An "X" chalked on the sidewalk indicated that the family who lived here probably was good for a handout; the Joynts' sidewalk was never unmarked.

In 1933, when Bob was eight, the name "Le Mars" made news across the country the morning after the town was rocked by farmers' anger. A run of bank foreclosures on Plymouth County farms struck the spark. Bob well remembered the day five hundred enraged farmers stormed the county courthouse, demanding that Judge Charles Bradley suspend all further foreclosures until recently passed laws regarding foreclosures could be considered. When the judge refused, the crowd rushed the bench, slapped Judge Bradley, tied him to a post, placed a rope around his neck, a hub cab on his head, and threatened to kill him. Wiser heads prevailed and the judge was released, never to serve on the bench again. For the farmers, administering a law that was being unfairly applied was not to be tolerated.[3]

For the most part, though, Le Mars was peaceful. Dr. Robert J. Joynt, III, a physics professor at the University of Wisconsin, sums up the culture of those years as he heard it from his parents and grandparents: "Northwest Iowa was very egalitarian then. The worst sin was putting on airs, or considering yourself superior to other people." Those who knew our Dr. Bob can see how perfectly he was the very image of this democratic model.

🌾 🌾 🌾

If anything marked Bob's father's family (three doctors, a dentist, and three nurses) more than medicine, it was laughter, a love of learning, and sharp wit. As Bob said: "My father had a fabulous memory. His greatest feat was the memorization of poetry, all the great American, British, and Irish poets. He always ended his recitations with 'Casey at the Bat' or 'The Shooting of Dan McGrew.'" "Doc" tried to impart this facility to his children, mostly on long car trips. "We started with the forty-eight states and their capitals," Bob remembered. "We then learned all the US presidents in sequence. However, the sockdolager[4] was to name the ninety-nine counties in abecedarian order along with their county seats. That never took with us."

Medicine as a profession was a Joynt family occupation—and preoccupation. A *Neurology* reminiscence written by Dr. Bob in 2009 no doubt is colored by hyperbole, but the spirit of the story is true.

> The high spot of the family reunions back then was finding out whether you needed your tonsils out or some teeth pulled. My father was a dentist and three of his brothers were doctors;

they all brought rudimentary extracting and excision equipment with them. The kitchen and ironing board served as the operating suite. Post-op, we were given ice cream and we all survived. Maybe this is the answer to the health care crisis.

Bob's father was locally famous for having served as the Democratic chairman of Plymouth County for thirty-three years. "Being a Democrat in Iowa at that time was a little like being Yassir Arafat at an Israel bond rally," his son has said. A gregarious bon vivant who lived up to the temperance pledge he took at his first communion, "Doc" Joynt was a popular, funny, and deeply involved participant in the life of Le Mars. At his retirement party, he claimed, "I've spent more time in smoke-filled rooms than a Virginia ham."

For Bob's wife, Margaret, who grew up in a neighboring town, two characteristics marked the Joynt family interactions: their devotion to each other and the respectful obedience the children showed their parents. "Never a raised voice," she recalls, and never, ever physical punishment. This at a time when "a trip to the woodshed" or a sound spanking was far from uncommon. A look of disappointment on the face of either parent or a word of reproach was punishment enough for the Joynt children. Amazingly, all four children always insisted there was never disagreement or squabbling among them.

⁊ъ   ⁊ъ   ⁊ъ

In another of his monthly comments in *Neurology*, Dr. Bob recalled hearing his parents frequently repeat homely remarks such as these:

> Father: *"Forty hours a week? What happened to working on Saturdays? . . . Thirty-five miles an hour is just about right. . . . If it hurts, rub a little dirt in it. . . . [A neighbor] must be all right. She's been through the Mayo Clinic."*

> Mother: *"Here, have another dessert. I made too much. . . . Why would you ever want to prepare food any other way than fry it? . . . Skimmed milk? What would you use that for? . . . Now, pin the dollar to your underwear."*

⁊ъ   ⁊ъ   ⁊ъ

Little Bob took to books almost as soon as he could hold one, according to his sisters. "He always had a list of books he wanted for Christmas," said sister Patty. "On Christmas morning, as soon as he unwrapped a book he would leave the Christmas tree, go over to a corner, and start reading. Mother would go to Sioux City to get books for him." This passion for reading seems to have been unique to Bob within the family. Bob's wife Margaret said there were few books in the Joynt house during Bob's early years, perhaps the result of the family's tight Depression-era budget.

Unfortunately, the eye problems that would plague Bob throughout his life began early. Measles, and the then-obligatory weeks spent in a dark room, left him with a turned-in eye; eventually it straightened, but from then on his eyesight was weak. "He wore glasses from an early age," remembered Patty, "but that didn't deter him from looking at every book he found." When a schoolmate teased Patty about her "four-eyed little brother," she hauled off and hit the kid in the nose. ("I hope it's still bleeding," she said many years later.)

The Carnegie Public Library in Le Mars was a magnet for the young boy. Back at home, in his own special spot, he would slip into his favorite reading pose, rump backward, legs draped over the back of the chair. He once told his parents, "I think I'll read every book there." He may have come close to doing just that.

Here's an odd fact. The man who would become a renowned physician, editor, dean, and distinguished professor flunked kindergarten. Well, not exactly; he *rejected* kindergarten. Bobby Joynt, even at five years old, seems to have required more "brain food" than most small-town preschool teachers could provide, and his thick glasses made him uncomfortable with rambunctious farm kids. "Never mind, Bobby. You can stay home this year," said mother Mayme. The following September, when his first-grade classmates asked why he'd left their kindergarten class, his answer was simple: "I graduated."

Young Bob's appetite for substantive conversation may be reflected in a rare rebellion: he stubbornly refused to have his hair cut. "If that kid doesn't get his hair cut soon, we're going to have to get him a dog license," his father once said. Asked why he was so resistant, Bobby answered: "Those barbers don't have anything constructive to say."

If kindergarten was a bust, Bob flourished through all the other grades. His entire classroom education, K–12, took place in *one* building. That may sound restricted, but he soon discovered a cadre of kids whose intellectual curiosity matched his own. As a member of Le Mars High School class of '44, Bob was one-fourth of a remarkable quartet of classmates who would become internationally known. The foursome of friends included our Dr. Bob; Dr. Thomas Starzl, chief of surgery at the University of Pittsburgh and a pioneer in kidney and liver transplants; Dr. Warren Stamp, chair of the Department of Orthopedics, University of Virginia; and Dr. Alvin ("Bud") Mauer, chair of pediatrics at the University of Indiana and former director of St. Jude's Cancer Center.

Other close school friends in Le Mars also grew up into illustrious careers. Curtis Harnack was a writer and former president of Yaddo, the artists' colony in Saratoga, New York, and Carlton Harker was the founder and president of a company that provides accounting and actuary services for hospitals nationwide, including the American Association of Surgeons. What was it about the school in that town of five thousand that produced such outstanding graduates? Someone has suggested, "Great Depression determination." Nothing in those days was easy, nor was it expected to be.

School wasn't all study, though. There were dates and dances, and drumming in the high school band. In later years, Bob clearly was quietly proud of his prowess on the high school football team. Although physically short and lacking depth perception, he was fast and determined. "He was a terrific passer," recalls Tom Starzl, "and I was a good catcher." With Bob as right halfback and Starzl at tight end, the team not only fought their way to a 7–3 record but also won the conference championship. "Bob was so fast [and shifty], we called him 'Mouse,'" wrote Starzl.[5] "We claimed that he was the only legally-blind passer in the state of Iowa. We should have added the most courageous."

❧   ❧   ❧

As the calendar turned to 1944, Bob saw his high school days coming to a close. All interest in other activities was overshadowed by news of the war raging in Europe, a conflict that was now, finally, America's war too. Across the nation, thousands of men and boys were being drafted; thousands more were volunteering, leaving factories, farms, schools and colleges, families and friends, to go wherever Uncle Sam would send them.

One day that spring, Bob Joynt and a friend drove to Omaha with plans to enlist in the army; both were rejected on physical grounds. A few weeks later, the boys tried again and were successful. By early June, both were privates undergoing basic training at Fort Dodge in Des Moines. Later that month, at the Le Mars High School graduation, more than one lad was missing from the jubilant crowd of seniors. When the name of the class valedictorian was announced, it was mother Mayme Joynt who proudly stepped up to accept Private Joynt's diploma.

2

SERGEANT JOYNT IN INDIA

The whole world, it seemed, was at war in the summer of 1944. Tens of thousands of lives were being lost every month, both in the Atlantic and Pacific theaters. Early in June, the first V-1 German rockets, launched from Cherbourg, landed on embattled London. By July, American and German blood was staining French farmers' fields as the relentless "battle of the hedgerows" wore on. On the other side of the world, kamikaze suicide bombers continued to destroy US aircraft carriers and their convoys marshalling in the South Pacific.

Promising signs, however, suggested that the war was beginning to turn in the Allies' favor. In Italy, Florence was liberated, although fierce fighting continued in the north; in France, the Germans were forced to retreat from Rennes, leaving another historic city in partial ruins. In the Pacific, US Marines landed on the islands of Guam and Tinian; after fierce fighting, Tinian would become the base for unrelenting bombing raids on mainland Japan.

Back at Fort Monmouth, New Jersey, a young signal corpsman from rural Iowa soon would be rolling up his sleeve for a series of exotic vaccinations—protection for a military assignment to a destination as yet unknown.

જ   જ   જ

Who could have guessed that the drum Bob Joynt's mother bought for him in high school would shape his military career? He claimed it did. During a skills test administered to new soldiers at Fort Dodge, Iowa, an officer noticed one young recruit's manual dexterity, honed, Bob believed, by hours spent learning to tap out jazzy rhythms with his cherished drumsticks.

When military brass noted that Private Joynt, novice radio telegrapher, scored high at sending and receiving codes, he was transferred to the Army Signal Corps Center at Fort Monmouth for advanced training. That skill may have been a lifesaver; it kept him out of the infantry and got him into the Army Signal Corps. Private Joynt's first trip east on a troop train was an eye-opener. "For the first time, I met a Jew—and then an Italian," Dr. Bob would say later. When one of his new buddies suggested they leave the base for supper, Bob was too shy to admit he had no idea what "going for a pizza" meant. Nor, later, did he know exactly why he was ordered to appear at the post's medical office to begin a series of vaccinations.

He soon found out. In April 1945, newly minted Staff Sergeant Joynt was aboard a ship escorted by destroyers, headed for Calcutta via Australia, a voyage that would take thirty-three days. When the ship docked briefly in Australia, Bob stepped off the boat, only to be ordered back on board by the military police. "I just want to be able to say I've been to Australia," he explained. The ship took the long route around Australia's south coast, hoping to avoid enemy submarines. Sergeant Joynt may have been one of the few on board who resisted the lure of the ever-present poker games, choosing instead to soak up the ship's library. A photograph of Bob, book in hand, sitting tipped back with his feet on the ship's rail, is evidence of how he spent most of his free time during these long weeks at sea.

On April 15, somewhere out on the ocean, a telegraph flashed the news that Franklin Delano Roosevelt had died at Warm Springs, Georgia. Even though most Americans knew of the president's post-polio weakness, the news was shocking. FDR had dominated America's political scene for thirty-two years. "I looked around and everybody was crying," Bob later told his wife. "He was the only president we knew." Pilloried by many Republicans, the man who in many ways epitomized the East Coast old guard was revered by most Democrats. Among them were the members of the Joynt family, who believed that FDR almost single-handedly had pulled the country out of the Great Depression by forcing passage of his New Deal social legislation. Now, a new commander in chief was in charge at the White House: Harry Truman. "Who's he?, we wondered," Bob recalled later.

🐾   🐾   🐾

Finally, after long weeks at sea, the contingent from Fort Monmouth reached India. As they made the trip by rail up along the Ganges River to Delhi, Sergeant Joynt must have been wide-eyed at his first sights of the exotic East, a world so vastly different from his beloved Iowa countryside. His first posting was at a telegraph station outside the city, where, in his spare time, he began studying Hindustani. (The Joynt children remember their father singing a Hindi lullaby as he escorted them upstairs to bed when they were young.)

Soon after his arrival in India, Sergeant Joynt was seconded to the British Army.[1] The previous year, former Field Marshal Archibald Wavell had been appointed commander in chief and viceroy of India. Wavell's charge was to strengthen the image of British imperial power—and track the movements of the Indian national army, then in the early stages of its revolt against the British Raj. For Wavell, a veteran of the African campaign, the times were not auspicious: locally, Bengali farmers were starving after years of drought; to the east, allies of Imperial Japan were seen as a potential threat. Most challenging of all for the British was the growing strength of the Quit India campaign, led by Mahatma Gandhi, the country's spiritual and de facto political leader.[2]

For the American telegrapher and his cohorts, working for Wavell meant joining a cat-and-mouse game, tracking the nationals' movements, locating their transmitting stations, and attempting to predict their plans. On Sundays, Wavell would invite some of his team to swim in the pool at his residence, a group that often included the Yank, Staff Sergeant Joynt.

Perhaps Wavell's mission was the reason that, for some of his time in the East, the Yank was on the move. He was in Peshawar, he went to Afghanistan, he visited the Taj Mahal. He spent time in New Delhi, where one afternoon he stood wide-eyed and amazed by one of Britain's great displays of imperial power: Lord Mountbatten and the viceroy leading a seemingly endless royal parade, complete with camel corps, elephants, bagpipes and bands, and British brigades marching in lockstep with their colorful flags and uniforms.

This grand display of colonial might no doubt was *very* impressive. But for Sergeant Joynt, it stood in stark contrast to life at the rural telegraphy post, "where the first one at the latrine in the morning had to sweep out the cobras." (This report comes directly from our young man from Iowa, who on occasion was obliged to lead the dawn's anticobra charge.)

🐾 🐾 🐾

On August 6, 1945, the Boeing B-29 "flying fortress" Enola Gay lifted off from the US Air Force base on Tinian in the Mariana Islands and headed northwest toward Japan. Its mission that day would shock the world into the Atomic Age—and leave Hiroshima, a city of 350,000 people, incinerated. (President Harry Truman had warned Japan's leaders to surrender or expect a continued rain of destruction from the air "the like of which has never been seen on this earth.")

Nine days later, Sergeant Joynt was at his post when the following teletype message came through, with orders to forward it immediately to President Truman: Imperial Japan had surrendered. Here was the news millions of Americans had been waiting for, and soon the V-J Day party was underway. On August 28, the Allied powers began occupying Japan. Five days later, with the principal signatories arranged on the deck of the battleship USS *Missouri*, Japan's surrender papers officially were signed. Finally, World War II was over.

For Sergeant Joynt, and millions of other servicemen and service women around the world, it was time to go home.

3

BECOMING "DR. BOB"

Here's how Bob liked to tell the story:

When I came back home from the army in 1946, almost the first thing my mother and father asked me was, "What are you going to do now, dear?"

Bob: *"Well, I love history and English literature. And I really liked working as a surveyor that summer. . . ."*

Mother: *"That's fine, Bob. You can do all that after you get your medical degree. . . . Now, what medical school do you want to go to?"*

Father (explosively): *"Iowa, of course! Where else?"*

And that, Bob Joynt would tell people later, that is why I became a doctor!

❧   ❧   ❧

Of course. Look at the family pattern. Steeped in medicine (and not just the men but the women who shared their lives as well). Bob's father, a dentist. Three uncles, doctors. Three aunts, nurses. And all with a strong connection to the University of Iowa. Uncle Mike was Bob's special pal, a general practitioner, the kind you can see in black-and-white movies from the '30s. Dr. Mike, who started practice in the horse-and-buggy era and, over the course of a fifty-year career, delivered 3,300 babies and wrapped who knows how many sprained wrists and ankles.

Now, in 1946, Bob was back again in Le Mars after spending eighteen momentous months in India, at the edges of a bloody war that had torn the world apart. No longer a boy after his two-and-a-half years of military service, but still just as eager as the kid who'd enlisted early, leaving his mother to pick up his high school diploma—and his valedictorian certificate. So, how ya 'gonna keep 'em down on the farm, after they've seen the wonders of Delhi? . . . The first step on the former staff sergeant's steep upward climb: get that undergraduate degree. What more convenient place to reenter the world of academia than next door at Westmar College, whose campus was not far from the Joynt family home. Founded in the late 1800s as both a normal school and business school, Westmar by the 1950s had grown to include over one thousand students. By living at home and walking the mile and a half to the campus, Bob was able to save his GI Bill benefits for his next big challenge: medical school.

Already a devout Catholic, Bob must have learned to tolerate Westmar's strong Protestant bias; a few years earlier the college had become an outpost of the Evangelical United Brethren Church. However, an even earlier merger with York College in Nebraska assured a certain diversity on campus, attracting students to Le Mars from throughout the Northwest. A naval aviation cadet program begun during World War II added to the mix of undergraduates.

Westmar's rules were rigid (no lipstick could be seen on the girls who lived in one of the college's two dormitories) and chapel was compulsory for the young church members. Not for Bob, though. "Bob and a friend would pack their clubs in the back of the car and take off for the golf course," his wife Margaret remembers. Fast on his feet, but too short to play college football, he slipped—ticket-less—into football and basketball games with his friends, the coach's sons.

Bob was a young man in a hurry. He studied German and all the other courses he would need to enter medical school, and somehow found time to serve as editor of the college's literary journal. By working his way nonstop through Westmar's syllabus—twenty-four months straight—he was ready to graduate in June 1949. His degree: BA, magna cum laude.

Years later, Dr. Joynt was invited back to Westmar to give the graduation address. That day he directed his speech not just to students but to the entire audience as well. His foil was Dr. Gradgrind, the nasty teacher in Charles Dickens's *Hard Times*, who insists that *facts* alone are important in teaching. For Gradgrind, students are "little vessels arranged in order, ready to have imperial gallons of facts poured into them until they are full to the brim. Teach nothing but facts. Root out everything else." Nonsense, the newest recipient of the college's honorary degree told the graduates. "At Westmar, I was given a healthy balance of fact and fancy. Facts for the outer world, fancy for the inner man. Always nourish the fancy. Take time out to read a book, see a play, listen to a concert, and sneak into a basketball game." It was a piece of advice that Bob Joynt knew by heart and always followed.

ᴈᴗ   ᴈᴗ   ᴈᴗ

The University of Iowa in September 1949 when Bob entered its medical school was a bustling place, academically and socially. Three hundred and twenty miles east of Le Mars, Iowa City was, by comparison, a metropolis. As was the university, with its fifteen thousand students, its gold-domed administration building, once the state's first capitol, and its leafy campus and rolling river. It was proud of its heritage: the first law school west of the Mississippi, first to award law degrees to a woman (1873) and to a black American (1879), a strong medical school and hospital, and a writers' workshop that would soon become renowned.

Like Bob, hundreds of new UI students were GIs eager to take advantage of the Servicemen's Readjustment Act of 1944. Over the next ten years, more than five million ex-servicemen would take advantage of the bill, creating in effect a new American middle class. Among its many offerings, the GI Bill, as it was called, provided free tuition at college or trade schools for servicemen returning from World War II. For Bob that meant four free years at medical school, free tuition, room and board, textbooks, and twenty-five dollars a week.

At UI, a fraternity and sorority system was in full flower at the undergraduate level. "Bob would never have joined a social fraternity," said his wife Margaret. He did, however, join Phi Beta Pi, one of four medical fraternities on campus; each had its own house and cook. The cook Bess Watkins hired Bob as her purchasing agent, and for seventy-five dollars a month he bought all the food and household supplies required for the always-hungry medical students.

Saturday night coed parties at the house often included hilarious pantomime skits, "flicker flashbacks," acted in stilted silent-movie fashion by Bob and his fellow medical students, to the amusement of campus friends. Rife with newly acquired medical knowledge and fully aware of all its raunchy possibilities, the young testosterone-inspired actors and skit writers were held in check by Bob. His silent "thumbs up, thumbs down" judgments, levied before the audience arrived, always were honored—yet somehow, the high humor of the skits' ridiculous antics was never diminished.

Those med school friends—his longtime Le Mars school pal Warren Stamp, Tom Dorsey and Jack Posnick from Fort Dodge, Iowa, and later Jim Milliman, Lynn Frink, and Bayard French— were a close-knit band, bright, funny, and all of them dedicated to their goal of becoming doctors. They studied together, they played together, and they dreamed together of what the future would hold. For Bob, that future was inextricably linked to Margaret McGivern, a law student who'd grown up in Marcus, the little town near Le Mars.

For Bob and other rabid sports enthusiasts, these were particularly heady days at UI. The young man who years later would celebrate the annual arrival of football season by tossing his black doctor's bag to an unsuspecting medical student with the command "Catch!" was in the right place at the right time. The legendary coach Forest Evashevski was about to lead the Hawkeyes to a new pinnacle of success, culminating in both a "Big 10" championship and a Rose Bowl win that would lift Iowans to a feverish level of excitement.

Coach "Ev" was a hero to all Iowa in the '50s. But it was another fine UI athlete who would shape Bob Joynt's postgraduate years. Adolph Sahs had been the red-hot first baseman on the Hawkeyes' varsity baseball team in the 1920s. Torn between his love of sports and the challenge of medicine, Sahs chose the latter—and in so doing would become one of the great men of neurology. A superb diagnostician and an outstanding teacher, Dr. Sahs was one of the "Four Horsemen" (along with A. B. Baker, Frank Forster, and Russell DeJong) instrumental in the founding of the American Academy of Neurology.

UI's medical school during Bob's years there had a well-established reputation for certain specialties: neurology, of course; ophthalmology; ear, nose, and throat; and—focused at the campus on the other side of the Iowa River—psychology and psychiatry; the latter discipline would have a special influence on the young medical student. Of the three neurologists on the faculty, A. H. Sahs would soon be nationally prominent, Thomas Summers would practice neurology in Des Moines, and Robert Utterbach would chair the department at the University of Tennessee.

According to Bob, however, it was his first-year anatomy professor, W. R. Ingram, who inspired his interest in basic science. Dr. Ingram, chair of the Department of Anatomy, was a brilliant teacher who introduced his first-year students to the mysteries of the brain. A pioneering anatomist, Ingram's work at the University of Chicago and the University of Iowa led to a more detailed understanding of the motor structure of the thalamus and midbrain, targets that Bob would pursue in his own early research.

At last, in 1952, the four years of grueling study by UI's fourth-year medical students were coming to a close. In 1951, Bob Joynt had been inducted into Alpha Omega Alpha, the honorary medical society; the next year he was tapped for Omicron Delta Kappa, the national leadership honor society.

That June, in sizzling early summer weather, families began gathering in Iowa City from across the state and beyond. For many of them, graduation day would be not only public recognition of their sons' achievements, but also of the years of skimping and saving that had made this day possible. At the baccalaureate service, Bob's parents and fiancée Margaret watched with pride as the family's fifth "Doctor Joynt" was awarded the Murchison MacEwen Prize as the University of Iowa Medical School's valedictorian and outstanding graduate student. Pomp and circumstance, indeed. But this time, unlike at Le Mars High School, Bob was there to accept the honor in person.

Graduation day itself must have been thrilling, not only for its emotional tenor and happy shine—the congratulations, parents' proud tears, and the graduates' shouts of joy—but also for what it presaged. In a few weeks the new Dr. Joynt would pack his suitcase and head north, leaving Le Mars and Iowa City for Montreal. There he would begin his internship at McGill University's Royal Victoria Hospital, then as now one of Canada's foremost medical science centers.

4

UNRAVELING NEUROLOGY'S GORDIAN KNOT

Montreal, Canada

A round 333 BC, Alexander the Great was conquering his way west across Asia when he reached a small town in Phrygia, now western Turkey. There the locals showed him a much-revered relic: an ancient oxcart tied to a post with a knot of great complexity. No one, the Phrygians believed, could ever untie this knot, fashioned long ago by Gordias, their early peas-ant-king, whose effort had been blessed by the gods. "Never" was the wrong word to use with the Great Alexander. With one blow of his sword, the knot was severed—and entered history as a symbol of a fast, effective way to deal with an intractable problem.

The art and science of neurology spurns Alexander's brutal approach. Its servants work instead to understand and relieve disturbances of the mind/body relationship using an approach that even their counterparts in other specialties view as "elegant."

Montreal, 1952

The two-toned green Ford rolled across the late June landscape, traveling eastward from Iowa across four states, finally crossing into western New York just south of Buffalo. Fresh off the factory line, the car rolled smoothly past farmlands, as if eager to be on the road, as eager as the cows it passed were to browse on the rich spring grass, free again after a winter in their cold, dark barns. The Ford hummed past acres of apple orchards on old Route 20, the trees' blossoms gone, their fresh green leaves newly unfurled.

Finally, somewhere near Syracuse, the Ford turned sharply north, heading for the Canadian border.

The car, a graduation gift from the driver's proud parents, wasn't allowed to dally. The man at the wheel had both a deadline and a destination: he had to be at Montreal's Royal Victoria Hospital by July 1, ready to begin his medical internship. There was another reason for his eagerness: He knew that Montreal was a hotbed of neurological research, that scientists there were involved in some of the most exciting research on the planet. They were trying to untie a Gordian knot, a neurological puzzle that needed to be taken apart, strand by tangled strand. Each piece of new information revealed would put them a step closer to unlocking the mysteries of the human brain. And that's *exactly* what interested young Dr. Bob Joynt.

Dr. Bob knew he was facing a challenge. All internships are grueling; this one would take place in an environment totally new to him, in which English was often the second language. His Westmar College French was almost adequate, but he was far from fluent. Everything would be strange in Montreal, everything would be unlike Iowa. Everything, that is, but the basic environment: a teaching hospital. *That* he knew something about. The rest he would learn.

When the Ford's driver finally pulled up in front of the Royal Victoria Hospital, he must have been impressed. What was this? Had some grand Scottish baronial castle been erected on the green, forested slope near historic Mt. Royal? A veritable mountain of gray Montreal limestone, the Royal Vic appeared to have been created by architects immersed in the culture of Sir Walter Scott's historical novels, still popular in 1893, the year the hospital was built. With its romantic turrets and crenellations, the vast, eight-story edifice in front of him was indeed a late-nineteenth-century wonder.

Functionally, in fact, much of the form of the massive complex was up-to-the-minute, inspired by the Crimean War nurse-reformer Florence Nightingale's recommendations for a modern hospital. Its multiple discrete patient pavilions were designed to discourage the spread of disease, patient rooms were airy and filled with light, and the whole complex was situated within a leafy, country-like environment—which was what the borough of Ville-Marie was at that time.

The railroad-magnate cousins Donald Smith and George Stephen, Scottish immigrants (newly titled Lord Strathcona and Lord Mount Stephen) whose million-dollar gift made the hospital possible, must have been pleased; they would later give a second million to endow the venture. The grand new hospital, free to all "of any race or creed," was dedicated to Queen Victoria, just beginning the fiftieth year of her reign. Around the world, Her Majesty's patriotic subjects were celebrating the occasion with pomp and circumstance. This grand new hospital would ensure that Montreal's homage to the sovereign would be fittingly impressive.

~ ~ ~

When Dr. Bob arrived in Montreal that day in 1952, the Royal Vic was already a revered institution. From the moment of its opening, the hospital was considered by many (certainly by all Canadians) to be the finest and best-equipped hospital in North America. Buttressed by its affiliation with nearby McGill University, the hospital had quickly acquired an international reputation for excellence in all three legs of the stool that represent good medicine: teaching, clinical care, and research.

As glorious as it was to be starting a new adventure, the thoughts of the young doctor often turned back to Iowa and to Margaret McGivern, the fiancée he was leaving behind; she would spend these next long months at UI, finishing work on her law degree. Next summer, finally, they could be married.

For twelve months Bob Joynt lived inside the Royal Vic, seeing patients throughout the day and night, studying, learning, trying to get through the grueling endurance course that is a rotating medical internship. Praying he wouldn't make a bad mistake. He would be paid no money, although he was given free room, board, and laundry service. The work was tough and seemingly endless. "I'm so exhausted tonight I can hardly think," Bob wrote to Margaret in one of the daily letters they exchanged.

Unfortunately for our story, there are few specifics on record for that year in Bob's life. We know that his three-month rotation in OB/GYN was almost unendurable (although he relished one wild ambulance ride, careening through narrow streets to aid a *femme enceinte* about to give birth.) We know that our young sportsman thought for a while that he really should learn to ski while he was up here in this winter wonderland. A few encounters with the truckloads of skiers arriving at the hospital with broken arms, legs, backs, and heads put an end to that pipe dream.

Dr. Bob decided to just keep working. Maybe now and then, if he was lucky, he could catch a few winks of sleep.

🙚   🙚   🙚

Yes, Bob was thrilled to be interning at the Royal Victoria Hospital. But there was another reason why he had been eager to be chosen as one of its new interns: the presence nearby of Wilder Penfield, acknowledged as one of the world's greatest neurophysicists and neurosurgeons. The brilliant Penfield was deeply involved in trying to unlock the mysteries of the human brain. Back in Iowa City, Professor Ingram's classes in anatomy and physiology had inspired a similar goal in his student. The fact that Penfield and his team were working right next door to the Royal Vic at the illustrious Montreal Neurological Institute was stimulating.

A Princetonian and Rhodes Scholar, Wilder Penfield had spent three years at Oxford in the second decade of the nineteenth century, studying mammalian physiology under the tutelage of the world's most famous neurophysicist, Sir Charles Sherrington, and clinical medicine with the equally eminent Sir William Osler. In 1918, with his medical degree from Johns Hopkins in hand, Penfield continued his studies abroad, working first in Germany on advanced surgical methods, in Spain on nerve-staining techniques, and in Boston as a surgical apprentice to the famed brain surgeon Harvey Cushing. (Wounded when his ship was torpedoed in the English Channel during World War I, Penfield recuperated at the home of Dr. Osler.) His resume, as you can see, was pure gold.

Penfield had set a personal goal: to establish a neurologic center that would combine basic research on the brain with hands-on clinical practice. By the late '20s, he had worked out a fully developed plan for such a center and was ready to move on it. Originally designed for Manhattan, his proposal there met with stiff and unrelenting opposition from that city's neurological community.

Undeterred, Penfield looked further afield. Invited to come north to Canada to discuss his plan with the president of McGill University, he brought with him the promise of $1.2 million in funding from the Rockefeller Foundation. Not only was he welcomed, but additional funds were also provided by Quebec's provincial government, the city of Montreal, and private donors. The Rockefeller grant stipulated that half its money be spent on building a neurology research center, the other half million on a hospital where patients with neurological problems would receive care.

In 1934, the Montreal Neurological Institute opened its doors, right next to the Royal Victoria Hospital, with Wilder Penfield its first director. Like the Royal Vic, the MNI was physically impressive: a conjoined complex of towering buildings, each capped by its own tall, tessellated roof. Formal, severe, impressive indeed. Throughout the '30s and '40s, Penfield, his colleagues, and his students investigated conditions across the neurological spectrum: epilepsy, brain edema, and neuromuscular diseases. A brilliant neural cartographer, Penfield developed the first large-scale functional map of the human cerebral cortex, precisely locating areas of the brain that control our movements, process our sensory experiences, and store our memories.

In the '50s, while Bob Joynt was interning at the Royal Vic, MNI scientists were deeply involved in research on epilepsy—especially on finding ways to treat patients with intractable symptoms. An outstanding neurosurgeon, Penfield found that, working with an epileptic patient under surgery, he could provoke the aura that warns of an upcoming epileptic attack. Then, using a mild electric current in the brain of the awake patient, he could locate the source of seizure activity and remove or destroy the offending tissue. More than half a century later, Penfield's "Montreal procedure" is still used as an investigative tool preparatory to further corrective surgery.

With other patients, Penfield discovered that by stimulating the temporal lobes on each side of the brain he could awaken memories repeatedly, including their specific sounds, movement, and color. Other investigations probed the puzzles of hallucinations and déjà vu experiences. Penfield wondered, could he, perhaps, even find evidence within the brain of the soul's existence? Like the young intern from Iowa, Penfield was fascinated by the brain's complexities—and he was determined to find his way through its tangle of neural pathways.

🙚 🙚 🙚

Throughout the '50s and succeeding decades, MNI's basic scientists made one remarkable medical advance after another. At the same time, the institute's neurological patients—each sequestered in a prototypical long, white ward lined with rows of iron beds— were now and then beginning to be helped by that research.

Word of the multiple ways in which MNI's investigators were revolutionizing neuroscience filtered down to the Royal Vic's interns. There's no doubt that word of each new discovery made young Dr. Bob ever more eager to get on with the daily business at hand—and eventually into his own laboratory. Every Tuesday evening, after hours of work in the patient wards at the Royal Vic, Bob would walk over to the MNI and spend time there. We know of one particularly notable laboratory exercise: students were challenged to create a three-dimensional model of the human brain, with all its parts and some of its complicated circuitry. Now *that* was the right kind of job for Bob Joynt. He needed to study the physical brain itself—the way it works, and the effect of the cascade of consequences that occurs when the brain is damaged. Poor eyesight, he knew, would always keep him from becoming a neurosurgeon, but he could—and would—become a fine neurologist.

In August 1953, this critical year in Dr. Bob's journey ended. Twelve months in Montreal performing hard, lowly work in the shadow of brilliant researchers were over. Ahead, in just a few weeks, he would take the next step—a giant one. Thanks to Senator Fulbright and one of his scholarships, Bob would spend the next year moving beyond what he had learned about the brain and its physiology in Iowa City and Montreal. Now he was headed for another neurological mecca, the renowned physiological laboratories at Cambridge University.

UNRAVELING NEUROLOGY'S GORDIAN KNOT

Cambridge, England

Cambridge, England, 1953

When the SS *United States* finally docked in Southampton that September, several thousand weary passengers lurched down the gangplank, clutching each other for support as they exited the ship on unsteady sea legs. What had promised to be a grand adventure on America's newest, fastest, and most elegant ocean liner, our rival to Britain's *Queen Mary*, had turned out to be anything but grand. For five days the great ship had been buffeted by wild storms. Tempests had tossed up breakers that seemed to hit the boat from all points of the compass simultaneously. So volatile was the upheaval that the deck was off-limits; for Bob, who loved the sea, and who was taking the turmoil in stride, this was a disappointment. Most passengers were seasick, so was half the crew. All slept fitfully. It was, they were told later, the worst crossing of the season.

This was not what the newly married Dr. and Mrs. Joynt had anticipated when they left the pier at Manhattan. There had been a grand send-off party the night before, sponsored by the Fulbright Foundation, where they'd immediately made friends with other scholars heading abroad. At last, it seemed, there would be leisurely days at sea, time to savor the pleasures of the past month: Margaret's graduation from the University of Iowa law school; their wedding in Margaret's home town of Marcus, Iowa, where Aunt Martha Ament's creamed chicken and fruit salad was served to three hundred friends and family in the community room at Church of the Holy Name; and, finally, their honeymoon in the Rocky Mountains.

Now, queasy and unsteady as they left the ship, Bob and Margaret made their way to the train that would take them to the University of London and a week of orientation in the ways of academic life in the United Kingdom. The next morning's breakfast of powdered eggs did little to settle stomachs still churning from the rough crossing, a discomfort that would last for several days.

For first-time visitors, this was an inauspicious time to be coming to war-weary England. Eight years after Germany's surrender, signs of the destruction unleashed on London by Nazi buzz-bombs were still everywhere. Whole sections of the city were pockmarked by ruined buildings, there were craters where bombs had exploded around the Tower of London, and here and there barricades blocked traffic where war-damaged roads were being repaired. Some churches were missing their steeple, others had steeples but no naves. Food was scarce, and some was still rationed. Fresh fruit? Sorry, not today—and probably not tomorrow either. Most poignant were the "walking wounded": former servicemen, now missing an arm or a leg, carefully threading their way through the streets of London.

Amid all these interesting new sights, Dr. Joynt's mind remained focused on what lay ahead: a year of research and study at the renowned Cambridge Physiological Laboratory, one of the university's most celebrated components. A bastion of brilliance, including, in 1953, three Nobel laureates, the laboratory's scientists were making giant strides in advancing what was known about the human body and brain. Among the biggest newsmakers that year were the scientists James Watson and Francis Crick, who, working in Cambridge's Cavendish Laboratory, had just announced their discovery of the double-helix structure of the DNA molecule and its implications.

Throughout the 1950s, interest in neuroscience was exploding on both sides of the Atlantic. Once linked in an academic partnership, neurology (then still paired with internal medicine) and psychiatry (fueled by Freud's new insights) were splitting into distinctly different disciplines. Montreal had offered the young scientist from Iowa an environment that had stimulated his interest in basic science, specifically the human brain and its workings. Now, Cambridge University and its famed laboratories would offer him distinguished professors and an international group of fellow students.

ॐ   ॐ   ॐ

Several days after their arrival in London, we find Bob and Margaret in Cambridge, each with a single suitcase. For them, as for so many others, the city would be heaven on earth. Unlike London, Cambridge had escaped the bombing, and that September its celebrated charm is on full display. Bicyclists are everywhere, crowding the narrow streets, most peddling furiously: men in business suits, black-robed dons, children in throngs, their bike bells ringing warnings as their young riders race to school or to playing fields. Women with shopping baskets pedal more leisurely, but purposefully, anticipating a cup of tea and a chat with friends at The Whim tea shop. . . . And, everywhere, the stunning backdrop of Cambridge town itself sets the scene: the towers, spires, gates, gardens, bridges, and stones of the university, whose walls for hundreds of years have shaped the character of this precious piece of England.

Dr. and Mrs. Joynt quickly find living accommodations, two small rooms and a shared kitchen in an attached house at 81 Chesterton Road, with a view of the River Camp. The landlady Elsie Norman may be the best part of the arrangement. A widow, Mrs. Norman introduces the young couple to the complexities of life in postwar Cambridge: how to use the mysterious Aga stove, which shop might actually have some good food, and how to maneuver their way by bike or bus around the city. Something of a bluestocking, with friends among Cambridge's literati, Mrs. Norman urges the young bride to enjoy the cultural life of the town while her husband is at work in the laboratory. Not that Margaret will have much free time. As a new lawyer, she has enrolled in the postdoctoral program in international law, matriculating at Newnham College, one of Cambridge's two colleges for women, only a "thruppence" bus ride away.

Bob is enrolled at Gonville-Caius College, proud bearer of a centuries-old reputation as a promoter of both medical teaching and scientific inquiry. Founded as Gonville Court in 1348, the school had been rechartered and received its new name in 1557 through the generosity of its patron and director, the noted physician John Caius—who included the caduceus symbol in the new college's emblem.

❧   ❧   ❧

As he heads for his first day at the renowned Cambridge Physiological Laboratory, our Fulbright Fellow knows he is a fortunate man—and in just the right spot. The incubator of multiple advances in neuroscience since its founding in 1874, the CPL is now at home in a massive, bow-windowed five-story red-brick edifice built in 1914.

Overseeing the laboratory is the towering presence of Edgar Adrian, a sharp-nosed, rapier-witted Nobel laureate in physiology, who had shared the prize in 1932 with his elder Cambridge colleague, Sir Charles Sherrington. Their studies of muscle and nerve cells were groundbreaking, and the Nobel prize recognized the importance of their discoveries regarding the functions of neurons. (Two years later, Edgar Adrian would become the first Baron Adrian, still later, President of the Royal Academy, and eventually Chancellor of Cambridge University.) Well-known by Cantabrigians as one of the throng of black-robed cyclists peddling furiously through town, bent far forward with his nose to the wind, Professor Adrian is no reclusive scholar-monk. A superb after-dinner speaker and an expert fencer, he, with his wife, is as well-known among Britain's mountaineering community as among his scientific colleagues.

Spurred by his work with soldiers suffering from nerve damage and shell shock, Adrian had returned to Cambridge after World War I as Professor of Physiology, where his research on the electrophysiology of the brain had led to a new understanding of the delicate partnership between the brain and the nervous system. A serendipitous accident in 1928 had led Adrian to the discovery that nerve cells contain electricity. One day, while experimenting on the retina, he had arranged electrodes on the optic nerve of a toad. To his surprise, as he moved around his laboratory, he heard repeated noises coming through the loudspeaker attached to the amplifier used in the experiment. Those noises, he later said, "indicated that a great deal of impulse activity was going on. . . . I realized I was in the field of vision in the toad's eye and it was signaling what I was doing." Later, using a cathode ray tube, a capillary electrometer, and valves to measure thermal activity in cells, Adrian found he could track electrical impulses in nerves by amplification; eventually he was able to amplify the sound of nerve impulses by a factor of five thousand.

Professor Adrian was the first to isolate, and then monitor and chart, reactions from a single nerve fiber. After selecting a single end organ cell muscle from a frog and connecting it with its related single nerve fiber, he subjected the muscle cell to various pressures—finger pressure, pinprick, etc. Carefully observing the reactions, he noticed that when the end organ was stimulated, the nerve fiber showed regular impulses with a variable frequency. While the strength of the cell's response after frequent stimulation quickly faded, he saw that the nerve's transfer rate remained the same for a much longer period of time before declining. These and other experiments with encephalography did much to further the understanding of epilepsy.

In a striking example of how scientific knowledge advances along a sometimes far-reaching network of scholarly pathways, Lord Adrian's studies of how pain impulses are received in the brain prefigured the brain-mapping work pioneered in the 1950s by Wilder Penfield in Montreal.

➛ ➛ ➛

Finally, a week after arriving in England, Dr. Bob meets the man who will direct his fellowship at the CPL. A tall, rangy fellow, looking like a man more used to being outdoors than in a laboratory, Dr. Bryan Matthews, the son of the dean of St. Paul's (Christopher Wren's great cathedral in London), is at that time the world's authority on the epidemiology of Creutzfeldt-Jakob disease. As early as the 1920s Matthews had made enormous contributions to neurophysiology. A technological genius, the eponymous Matthews's Oscillograph was the first device to record nerve fibers carrying information to muscles. Another of his inventions, a differential amplifier, could record high-gain, low-noise electrical activity in biological systems—and is still widely used today in encephalography.

Friendly yet commanding, with a warm sense of humor, Dr. Matthews's public persona equaled his reputation as a scientist. During the war he had chaired the Royal Air Force Commission on Aviation Medicine—and, at this very moment in our story he is fine-tuning last-minute details for what would become Sir

Edmund Hillary's successful first ascent of Mt. Everest. Years later, as Sir Bryan Matthews, he would become editor in chief of the *Journal of Neurological Sciences,* the official journal of the World Federation of Neurology.

Impressive on all counts. But when Dr. Bob, the newest of the Fulbright Fellows, meets the eminent Dr. Matthews, the older man's greeting is friendly and simple: "Welcome! You'll find your lab at the end of the hall. When you figure out what you want to work on, let me know. We'll get you what you need. . . . Tea is at four." Dr. Bob has known from his medical school days in Professor Ingram's class what he wants to study: the hypothalamus, the hormone-producing part of the brain that regulates body temperature, thirst, hunger, sleep, moods, and the sex drive (a major multitasker). And what he needs are frogs, lots and lots of frogs.

In later years, at the University of Rochester, Dr. Bob (helped immeasurably by his secretary Nancy Baldwin) developed a remarkable personal records archive, ninety-five boxes now spread over forty-eight linear feet in the Miner Medical Library. Unfortunately, as was the case in Montreal, we have no precise record of how Dr. Joynt spent his days at the CPL. No mention of specific experiments, no lab notebooks, no lab drawings of frog brains, no transcripts, no written exchanges between the researcher and his research director. No summing-up report to the Fulbright Fellowship Committee. What we can be sure of is that Dr. Joynt was exploring what had first stimulated his interest back in Professor Ingram's anatomy class in medical school: What is the nature of the hypothalamus? How does it work? And what role does the nervous system play in carrying out that work?

We also can be sure, knowing the character of the young researcher, that he was indefatigable in his efforts, and that those efforts met with the approval of his research director, as noted by his official certificate of completion from the CPL. We know, too, that his research in the CPL would have an important academic payback: it fulfilled all the requirements for his master's degree back at the University of Iowa.

❧   ❧   ❧

Hard facts about Dr. Bob's research in Cambridge may be scarce, but Margaret's memories of those days are rich and varied. We can see the young couple, so strapped for cash they must share a single black sleeveless scholar's gown, the required uniform for classes and lectures, at required dinners at their respective colleges, and always on the streets at night. We see Bob Joynt, a man "on the short side of medium," on his way to a black-tie dinner in London at the Royal Academy of Medicine, unabashedly wearing a tuxedo borrowed from a six-foot-four friend, its cuffs rolled and loosely stitched up by Margaret.

The winter months in Cambridge are excruciatingly cold that year, and the Joynts' newest lodgings, at 1a Water Street, have no central heat. At night they draw chairs as close to the fire as they can; while the fronts of their legs turn beet red, the backs remain icy cold. There's culinary discomfort too. More than one dinner at Margaret's college consisted of boiled cabbage and potatoes (the very menu that Virginia Woolf had railed at fifty years earlier). This paupers' fare is the result of wartime scarcities, and both men's and women's colleges are suffering. While her husband is at the lab, Margaret is at the law library, preparing her own thesis, "The Nationality of Married Women."

Never mind the cold, gray, Spartan season. With the coming of spring, Cambridge is once again at its glorious best. Every college boasts spectacular gardens, the famous perennial borders of Cambridge springing from loam eight-feet deep, the rich accumulation of centuries. Their glory calls out to visitors, and the Joynts are eager to respond. On weekends, the young couple joins spring-feverish undergraduates, punting and picnicking on the River Cam. Together, Bob and Margaret stroll along "the Backs," the acres of greensward that border the banks of the river. By early May, Margaret is walking more slowly. On May 28, at about three in the afternoon, the family increases by one-third as baby Bob Jr. is born at Mill Road (Maternity) Hospital.

At Mill Road, the young parents experience firsthand Britain's new national health system. Upon the couple's early-morning arrival at the hospital, the concerned father, eager to be on hand for the baby's birth, is quickly—and insistently—dismissed. "Visiting hours begin at five," he is told. When he protests, the matron frowns: "Don't you have a job to go to?" Rebuffed, he returns to the lab, simmering. . . . At four o'clock, a five-pound note, slipped to a nurse, gains him admission. At last he is able to see his almost-newborn son. For Margaret, sharing a ward with four other new mothers, the new system provides ten full days of rest and care. Sixty years later, she remains full of praise for her experiences as a new mother with Britain's national health system.

☙ ☙ ☙

Now it is time for our young couple and their new baby to return home. Margaret is so well rested after her ten-day stay at Mill Road Hospital that she and Bob, always up for a party, host a farewell gathering at home for their friends from the laboratory. In turn, these friends present Bob with a handsome Sherlock Holmes-style Meerschaum pipe, a treasured token that through the years will have a prominent place on his office desk, first in Iowa City and then in Rochester, New York.

The trip back to America would happen only when a major challenge had been met successfully. British law required that the new baby could not leave Britain until he had been vaccinated for smallpox. His father's Fulbright-paid ticket home was dated June 24, well before those six weeks of waiting would be over. The dilemma was solved when Margaret was invited to stay with Cambridge friends until mother and baby could fly back to America.

So on June 24, 1954, Dr. Bob, traveling alone, boarded the *Queen Mary* and headed for home. Unlike "the trip from hell" that had brought the newlyweds to London, this was blue skies and clear sailing all the way. Ahead lay three years of residency in neurology back at the University of Iowa and a doctoral thesis to prepare. There, those little frogs and their pulsing brains would continue to figure large in Dr. Bob's professional life.

6

UNRAVELING NEUROLOGY'S GORDIAN KNOT

University of Iowa

Iowa City, 1954

Once again, it seems, young Dr. Bob was in the right place at the right time when he began his three-year residency at the State University of Iowa Hospitals on July 1, 1954. UI's Department of Neurology, established in 1919, has a distinguished history, preceded only by those at Harvard and Columbia; its neurology residency program was one of the first to be accepted by the American Board of Psychiatry and Neurology.

Clarence Van Epps, its initial director and first professor, had done postgraduate work in Philadelphia and Vienna. Over the course of his career, Dr. Van Epps would train more than fifty neurologists—and he remained a major presence during Dr. Joynt's residency. Wreathed in distinction, Van Epps must have seemed rather unapproachable to the young residents. Appearances are, of course, often misleading. Our young doctor was abashed the day he made an unfortunate mistake in Dr. Van Epps's presence. "Never mind, young man," said the professor. "Don't worry about mistakes, always go forward." With the thought of his error still stinging, Bob asked, "Dr. Van Epps, have you ever made a mistake?" After a very long moment, the professor replied, "Yes, in 1900, I voted for William Jennings Bryan." (Fifty years later, that "mistake"—voting for a Democrat in a presidential election in rock-solid Republican Iowa—obviously still rankled.)

When Bob began his postgraduate years at UI in 1954, he was a US Public Health Service Fellow in the Department of Neurology. For the next twelve years, he would begin building his career at the same university that had so influenced other members of his extended family. Working in the related fields of anatomy and neurology, he would leave his mark on the university. In turn, UI would forge the foundation of his own reputation as one of neurology's remarkable men.

❧ ❧ ❧

Is there any greater force in shaping a life than a professor who opens the door to the future for a student? For Bob Joynt, that professor was Dr. W. R. Ingram, his professor of anatomy. From his medical student days at UI, Bob recognized in this portly and imposing professor personal qualities that would come to characterize his own career.

His first personal encounter with Rex Ingram, Bob later recalled, was in "the dreaded anatomy oral examination," carried out in the presence of the cadaver. Bob was hoping the questions would be administered by one of the young surgical residents, but he was unsettled when he was sent for by the great professor himself. "I remember very little except that I could not identify the medial and lateral anterior nerves," he wrote later in an appreciation. "What I do remember best is the kindness and patience Dr. Ingram had. He knew the state of mind we were in and acted accordingly."

Dr. Ingram had a reputation among the medical students and residents as knowing more about the hypothalamus—one of Bob's own interests—than anyone in the world. A meticulous and deft surgeon, his neuroanatomy lectures were models of their kind, "so precise that, if recorded, they would need no editing for publication," Bob later recalled—no superfluous material, no repetitions, no personal anecdotes. Bob was so impressed that, before leaving UI to begin his fellowship in Cambridge, he had asked to work with Dr. Ingram on stereotaxic techniques, the delicate three-dimensional procedures that enable a surgeon to locate and treat lesions deep with the brain.

Now, his inspirational year at the Cambridge Physiological Laboratory complete, Dr. Bob was ready to start his clinical training and, when time permitted, to pursue his graduate studies under the tutelage of Dr. Ingram. In his published appreciation of his mentor, he recalls: "My work was on the hypothalamus, but it was an electro-physiologic study. Dr. Ingram was initially unfamiliar with this, but soon read everything he could on the subject. He often pointed out papers which were unknown to me and offered excellent criticism and lines to pursue. . . . One day I quoted some early work on *diabetes insipidus* done by Farmi. He said the name was Farini, and that I should read the original work and not the German paper which had consistently misspelled Farini's name. He was correct, and gently admonished me always to read the original presentations." It was a lesson in mentoring, indeed.

⁊⊷   ⁊⊷   ⁊⊷

Almost from the moment Dr. Bob began his residency, a wave of work swept over him. Neurology in 1954 was just beginning to be considered a medical specialty, and neurologists were few and far between; Des Moines, the state capitol, had none. At the same time, Iowa state law offered tertiary care to all its citizens. As a result, patients with low income who had neurological problems were being brought to the university hospitals by ambulance, at no charge, from throughout the state. For the two residents on call, that meant one or the other would spend alternate nights at the hospital, in addition to seeing patients during the day. Hard work for first-year residents, who were paid $300 a month.

As for Margaret, she was busy with a rapidly growing family: Bob Jr., born in Cambridge, was soon joined by Patricia in '55, Mary in '57, Ann in '59, Tom, '61, and Kathy in '64. Their home that first year of residency was in veterans' housing, a corrugated-metal, double-family dwelling, each unit heated by a pot-belly stove. For the Joynts, this arrangement had two great advantages: the rent (furnished), fifty-one dollars a month, and (even better) its location—a walkable mile to the hospital and a block from the football stadium. Every weekend during the fall, the family was surrounded by the sound of the Hawkeyes marching band and the noise of thousands of rabid fans, hootin' and hollerin'. For Bob, a former high-school running back and an avid sports fan, this was sweet music. Every home-game weekend, Margaret's parents would make the three-hundred-mile drive down from Marcus and join the young couple's friends from graduate days. "At game time, with a babysitter to watch the kids, we'd join the crowd," says Margaret. Everyone would have lunch and supper with Bob and Margaret, who always provided a moveable feast.

With the family expanding, the Joynts soon bought a house in a real neighborhood—three bedrooms and a big backyard lined with sweet-smelling mock-orange bushes. Together Bob and Margaret painted the cement floor of the sun porch black and red and, for seating, turned to that iconic fifties piece, the butterfly chair, choosing canvas covers in black and red. Social life was wonderfully casual: buffet dinners with fellow residents, students, and, as Bob progressed up the career ladder, faculty. From Dr. Ingram, Bob learned the importance of building ties with students, and Friday night pizza parties with Dr. and Mrs. Joynt became a ritual.

Time and funds may have been tight, but somehow there was always time for friendships that transcended departmental boundaries. The bibliophile David Green, an internist who later practiced in Albany, New York, had a mind as wide-ranging as Bob's own, and their exchanges of wit and wisdom were no doubt doubly salutary. Another close friend was Adel Afifi. Afifi had been sent to UI from the University of Beirut to take a neurology residency, a move designed to strengthen Beirut's neuroscience department. (Years later, Dr. Afifi would invite Dr. Bob to give the annual Wilder Penfield lecture in Beirut, and, in a friendly turnabout, Afifi would discuss Pick's disease at the University of Rochester.)

❧   ❧   ❧

Chairing the Department of Neurology at UI during these years was Adolph H. Sahs. Once again, Dr. Bob found himself working with another extraordinary mentor. Under Sahs's leadership, neurology as a specialty at UI would extend its national and international recognition, in no small part because of Sahs's multiple roles as a founder and president of the American Academy of Neurology, the American Board of Psychiatry and Neurology, and the American Neurological Association (all organizations that Dr. Bob later would lead).

An expert on subarachnoid hemorrhage and intracranial aneurysms, Dr. Sahs was a brilliant teacher who had the gift of simplicity in his relationships with students. As Dr. Bob would point out in his obituary for Sahs in *Archives of Neurology*, "although Dr. Sahs was eminently successful, he was devoid of any selfish ambition." Sahs's frequent advice to his students reflected his humanism: "If you have 30 minutes to see a patient, spend 29 on the history, one on the examination, and none on the EEG and skull X-ray." The technology could come later, he implied, after the physician had a real understanding of both the patient and the problem.

This humanistic point of view was being promoted at the same time at the University of Rochester, where John Romano, George Engel, and William Morgan were building a medical education program based on the importance of the physician understanding not just the disease but also how the patient's health is affected by his or her genetic and socioeconomic environment. Their biopsychosocial model would find a national following at other medical schools, and it is still promoted as an ideal through every level of medical education at the University of Rochester.

ᔛ   ᔛ   ᔛ

Throughout the years 1957–61, as an assistant professor and then as an associate professor, Bob continued working with both Ingram in anatomy and Sahs in neurology. No longer strictly focused on the hypothalamus, he became intensely interested in behavioral neurology, a subspecialty that examines the neurological basis of behavior, memory, and cognition. That interest was further sparked by his growing friendship with Arthur Benton, an innovative neuropsychologist working on UI's liberal arts campus. Bob encouraged Benton to strengthen his basic science credentials, and the psychologist earned an appointment in neurology at the College of Medicine. The IQ tests that Benton devised are still used by psychologists today. His book, *Exploring the History of Neuropsychology*, is dedicated to "my longtime friend and colleague, Robert Joynt, who is himself a distinguished historian of neurology."[1]

Both Benton and Joynt were intrigued with the problem of aphasia and how it relates to hemispheric dominance in the brain, a question that had been puzzling brain scientists since at least the mid-nineteenth century. Five papers by Dr. Joynt on aphasia written during the '60s reflect his growing interest in the subject, an interest both clinical and historical. A 1961 paper recalls the famous century-old case of "Tan," an aphasic patient at Bicêtre Hospital in Paris. This poor fellow, a patient of the famed neurosurgeon Pierre

Broca, could only voice the nonwords "Tan-tan," except under stress, when he would exclaim, "Sacre nom de Dieu!" By studying "Tan," Broca determined that the area of the brain responsible for articulated speech lies in the third-left frontal convolution. "We speak with the left hemisphere," Broca said—and the implication that other regions of the brain might control specific human functions created a storm of controversy. (Bob, writing about "Tan" a century later, surely saw the strong link between Broca's nineteenth-entury work and Wilder Penfield's twentieth-century "cerebral cartography" studies in Montreal.)

In 1960, Benton and Joynt invited four international neuroscientists to come to Iowa City to discuss questions of cerebral dominance, aphasia, amnesia, and related conditions: Henry Hecaen, from Paris; MacDonald Critchley, from Queen Square, London; Oliver Zangwill, from Cambridge; and Norman Geschwind, from Harvard. This was the first gathering of a group that would focus on cerebral dominance for the next two decades. Every three years they would gather at Iowa City, Zurich, Paris, or Lisbon. Joining them in later years were Drs. DiRienzi from Italy and Antonio Damasio from Portugal. The men, with their wives, become close friends, spending many laughter-filled evenings hosted at home, family style, in Iowa City and sampling European restaurant fare abroad.

In all, Dr. Joynt's name appears as first author or coauthor on thirty-eight papers published during his twelve years at UI. His first paper, coauthored with Dr. Sahs, was read in 1956 at the eighth annual meeting of the American Academy of Neurology in St. Louis. "Brain Swelling of Unknown Cause" reviewed twenty-seven studies of unexplained edema (one dating to 1897) and presented three of the cases in detail. The authors concluded that the etiology remained unsettled, although new radiologic and biochemical techniques might provide answers in the future.

The breadth of topics covered by Dr. Joynt in these papers is impressive, including epilepsy, electroencephalography, meningitis, aphasia, and others. In 1961 he was listed as first author, with Sahs, on a paper on meningitis; together they wrote the chapter on meningitis in the second edition of *Baker's Handbook of Clinical Neurology*. Dr. Joynt created a stir within the chiropractic community with his 1959 *JAMA* paper, cowritten with his UI colleague David Green: "Vascular accidents to the brain stem associated with neck manipulation." Their conclusion: Some people may have an abnormal vascular supply to the basilar arterial system that puts them at risk for this kind of physical manipulation." A paper that goes off in quite a different direction is "Meningitis," in *Traumatic Medicine and Surgery for the Attorney* (1961).

The late University of Rochester neurologist David Goldblatt recalled the 1961 paper that Dr. Joynt wrote with David Green on auscultation of the skull. "Green and Joynt listened with the diaphragm of the stethoscope over the site of a large osteolytic skull lesion and found that when the patient said 'Ninety-nine' it sounded clearer and higher-pitched than on the unaffected side. Phonocardiography substantiated their findings. 'Auscultation of the skull for differences in vocal resonance,' they suggested, 'may be helpful in the detection of large osteolytic lesions.'" A primitive method by today's standards, of course—and Bob later said he would be forever thankful that no one called their finding "the Green-Joynt sign."

🙚　🙚　🙚

But what about "the Big Paper"? Young Dr. Robert Joynt was making a name for himself as an author of note for scientific papers, a fine clinician, and an inspiring teacher. But his future in academic medicine required something bigger: a PhD thesis, written, defended, and published. As for the topic, Adolph Sahs and Arthur Benton encouraged him to focus on his research at Cambridge: hypothalamic water regulation and the osmoreceptor. Do it *now*, they urged.

The only way this was going to happen was for Bob to turn his attention to the task. That meant taking a year off from clinical work and teaching. And *that* meant no money would be coming in from the university to support this family with six children. To fill the financial gap, Bob took nighttime jobs reading EEGs and seeing patients at the VA Hospital. What remained of each twenty-four hours was *study, study, study; write, write, write.*

In 1963, Dr. Robert J. Joynt's thesis—"The electrical activity of osmosensitive units in the anterior hypothalamus and pituitary stalk of the cat"—was published. Its author used micro-electrodes to record and measure the electrical activity of units, presumably extracellular recordings of single cells, as they responded to various intracarotid injections of solutions that contained traces of a single drug, such as epinephrine, norepinephrine, nicotine, or morphine. The results tracked the degree of each drug's effect on the firing frequency of the units and on the release of antidiuretic hormone (ADH). In summary, the author concludes: "It would appear that several neural pathways converge in the anterior hypothalamus and not on the supraoptic nucleus. Some of these pathways may react in different ways to various pharmacologic agents. The final result is an integrated stimulus of the proper release of [ADH], so that the fluid exchange of the body is appropriate to its immediate internal and external environment."

❧   ❧   ❧

By the mid-60s, Bob Joynt's hard work was paying off. As the neuroscientist Ira Shoulson would write later in *Archives of Neurology*: "Word began to spread through academic neurology circles about the talented rookie who had far-reaching expertise from electroencephalography to meningitis, and interests from osmoreceptors to public policy."

Inevitably, the time would come for Bob Joynt to say farewell to the University of Iowa. Ahead, to the east, lay bigger challenges and greater responsibilities.

7

DR. BOB BUILDS A NEW DEPARTMENT

Let's let Dr. Bob, who became the Department of Neurology's first chair in 1966, explain in his own words why the neurology division had just been elevated to a free-standing department: "Neurology, which had traditionally been a rather small specialty, was munificently funded in the '50s and '60s through the then-named National Institute of Neurological Disease and Blindness. Money for research and training was more available to those schools where Neurology flourished as a major Division."[1] This fact was not unknown to the University of Rochester president Allen Wallis or to two successive deans and directors of the medical school during the '60s, Donald Anderson and Lowell Orbison. Their conclusion: If the federal government wanted to invest its resources in universities where neurology faculty worked within a discrete department rather than in just medicine, the University of Rochester would oblige.

The elevation of neurology to department status in 1966 was a major advance. The first neurologist to join the faculty was Paul H. Garvey, who had arrived in Rochester in 1928 when the medical school was only three years old. A graduate of Johns Hopkins, Garvey would lead the neurology division, a subsection of the Department of Medicine, until his retirement in 1963. Three years after Garvey's arrival, he was joined by his Hopkins colleague Wilbur Smith, a charismatic teacher of neuroanatomy and neurophysiology, many of whose students became nationally known. Together Garvey and Smith, aided by Drs. Sandra Feldman and Agneta Borgstedt, not only taught, conducted research, and saw patients, but also supervised an NIH-funded postgraduate training program in neurology.

Impetus for change in American medical schools was stimulated in the late '50s as interest in neuroscience intensified at universities—and in Washington. There was good reason for optimism.

Sponsored funding for research and research training at the UR Medical Center was growing. In 1950, the total in federal funding had just surpassed $2 million; by 1966, the year Dr. Bob arrived, it had grown to $10 million. In 1975, less than ten years later, it would reach the $22 million mark.

During the '50s, a group of UR scientists studying brain structure, organization, and function formed the Center for Brain Research, which became well regarded nationally. Looking to a future that was fast approaching, Dean Lowell Orbison appointed the influential faculty member George Engel, a psychiatrist and internist, to form a committee to investigate the impact of current advances in neurobiology on teaching, research, and practice at the University of Rochester.

The Engel Committee Report of 1960 stressed that, thanks to postwar advances in medical technology, an explosion of new knowledge was leading to a better understanding of how the nervous system directly affects the preservation of health—or the development of disease. Engel had concluded that, at Rochester, neurobiology was underdeveloped and should be the immediate focus of medical school planning. His committee envisioned a collaborative venture and sharing of resources between the Center for Brain Research and a new Department of Neurology.

Who would lead this important new venture? Engel chaired a select committee to seek out qualified candidates for the job. Robert Haggerty, the former chair of pediatrics, and a member of that committee, points out how important Engel's leadership was to the search. "George insisted that each of us should spend a couple of days observing a candidate on his own territory, talking to faculty colleagues and to students as well," he says. Haggerty himself visited a "hot-shot" researcher at Columbia, but soon realized that few of the residents and none of the students knew the man. "George's insistence that we visit candidates on site, rather than inviting them to Rochester, changed the whole tenor of the search [for the better]," he says.

It was George Engel himself who made the trip to Iowa City to meet the young man who was making a name for himself at the University of Iowa medical school: Dr. Robert J. Joynt, Jr. Even though Bob Joynt was a "rookie" compared with other candidates, he impressed his interviewer. "When George came back from Iowa, he told us that the students, residents, and faculty whom he'd talked with were all very enthusiastic [about young Dr. Joynt]," Haggerty recalls. And that was how Bob Joynt, in 1966, became chairman of the new Department of Neurology at the University of Rochester.

☙ ☙ ☙

"Margaret, I'm going to build the best Department of Neurology in the country." That's what Mrs. Joynt recalls her husband saying as the family drove across the country from Iowa toward their great new adventure. Over the next twenty-two years, Bob would take a program that began with three faculty members and turn it into what is now a nationally acclaimed educational and scientific powerhouse whose full-time faculty now number ninety-seven and where research funding tops $17 million annually.

What does it take to start a new medical department within the complicated environment of a first-class medical center? Bob Joynt often answered the question this way: "Hire people who are smarter than you—and then get out of their way." The young doctor from Iowa would follow his own advice. But he also had—in abundance—the simplest, often rarest, of tools: keen intelligence, uncompromising honesty, wit without parallel, skill at building friendships, a boundless capacity for hard work, and a faith-based openness to the world around him. Many young Rochester-trained physicians still carry with them his often-repeated counsel: "Remember! You can't always be right . . . but you can always be kind."

But what are your chances of succeeding when you're the new young man in town? It helps to have strong financial backing. Dr. Bob's great friend Dr. Joseph Martin, retired dean of Harvard Medical School and former dean and chancellor of the University of California, San Francisco, knows the importance of that kind of support. "I came to Rochester to do a postdoctoral fellowship in neuroendocrinology because I knew that Bob had been given the entitlement and resources to build a great department," he says. "He soon became my friend, colleague, and mentor."

The new chairman's job list was both long and clear. First, he had to recruit more faculty; some would need offices in which to see patients, others would need laboratories and equipment. He had to develop a strong residency program to train new neurologists. Secretaries, bookkeepers—support staff would be required to keep things running smoothly. And everything would cost money. He would have to keep it coming, and then look for more.

Paul Griner, the former CEO of Strong Memorial Hospital and now a medical consultant near Boston, remembers this time well. "I had the privilege of watching the Department of Neurology grow with the terrific recruitments Bob made," he says. "Over the seventeen years when I was running the hospital, the Department of Neurology grew to become one of the largest in the country and one of the most successful in terms of extramural support. Bob deserves the greatest share of the credit for that."

Child neurologist Gary Myers recalls the physical space the new department occupied in those first years. "Neurology's offices were in Q Wing, on the second floor near the medical school's original entrance on Crittenden Road. Bob had the big center office, but he didn't like the solid wood door that separated him from the rest of us. He had a university carpenter turn it into a Dutch door, so the top half could remain open, but was astonished when the $700 bill for the work arrived." Never mind—now his door was open to both students and faculty.

No medical department is a universe unto itself, and neurology traditionally has had particularly strong ties with pediatrics, psychiatry, and neurosurgery. Keeping those relationships running smoothly is important—and that was another of the new leader's talents. Dr. Bob built strong faculty ties with Frank Smith, director of the neurosurgical unit, and his team, Joseph V. McDonald and later Shige Okawara; with John Romano, the powerful chair of psychiatry; and with Robert Haggerty, the chair of pediatrics who, with a $3 million federal grant, opened five inner-city clinics in Rochester where medical residents would get real-life exposure to public health issues.

～ ～ ～

Patient care would be a primary focus for Dr. Bob. He had inherited as first faculty three outstanding neurologists, Richard Satran, David Goldblatt, and David Marsh; Paul Garvey, nearing retirement, saw patients on occasion. With the founding of the department, all had moved from medicine into neurology.

Soon a string of new appointments was underway. The new chair realized early that the new Rochester General Hospital, built to serve the city's north side, would need a neurology service, and he quickly saw the importance of building a partnership between the two hospitals. In 1969, he recruited Joshua Hollander from the University of Michigan to lead the program, and later added the former neurology resident Gerald Honch to the RGH team. The numbers of faculty grew with the arrival of the Medical Center's first child neurologist, Frederick Horner, a professor of both pediatrics and neurology. Horner soon was joined by David Van Dyke and Gary Myers, from Boston Children's Hospital; together they initiated a strong program in child neurology, now an important subspecialty.

But all these faculty needed patients to care for, teach around, and study. Fortunately, the Engel Committee had realized this and, in preparation for the change, arranged that patients with neurological problems in the Departments of Medicine and Pediatrics would be seen by neurologists; at the same time, Strong Memorial Hospital's rehabilitation unit also was transferred to the new department.

?◆   ?◆   ?◆

During the tumultuous '60s, changes in the nation's approach to health care had reshaped the hospital scene in Rochester. In 1965, the federal Medicare and Medicaid programs were initiated, and a new affiliation was formed between the University of Rochester and Monroe County to administer them. UR neurologists and trainees would soon be seeing many more patients.

When Dr. Bob arrived in Rochester in 1966, the massive Monroe Community Hospital (that architectural wonder!) was on the verge of transformation. This hospital, which served many of the community's indigent and those needing long-term care, would be energized by another new doctor in town, T. Franklin Williams, a "founding father" of geriatric medicine. In North Carolina, Williams had developed an interdisciplinary approach that would revolutionize patient care for this population. When Williams arrived in Rochester in 1968 as the new director of MCH, he and Dr. Bob soon formed an effective partnership.

The Strong Memorial/MCH partnership was a symbiosis of the best kind. Of the hundreds of patients at MCH, many had severe neurological problems. Faculty from the Department of Neurology—Marvin Goldstein, Robert Hamill, and Randolph Schiffer—soon were attending to their care *and* establishing research programs focused on their patients' special needs. A key recruit from Duke University was Guy Molinari, whose research on ways to prevent the aftereffects of stroke was promising.[2] On site at MCH too were increasing numbers of neurology residents who would learn to care for patients who desperately needed their help; several of the residents would be inspired to begin their own research in the emerging field of geriatrics.

Similar programs were underway at the Rochester General Hospital and at the Genesee Hospital in the center of the city. "Taking care of the folks" at RGH was Bob's job description for Joshua Hollander when he recruited the basic scientist from Ann Arbor in 1969. Hollander was soon joined by Gerald Honch (who had been recommended for the neurology residency program by Dr. Joynt's own mentor, Adolph Sahs at UI). Also beginning his career at RGH in those early years was child neurologist David Wang, still a key member of the neurology team and now at UR Medical Center.

At the time of the Department of Neurology's fortieth anniversary in 2007, Gerry Honch recalled his first days in Rochester as a resident. "At the right moment in my life, someone took an interest in me," he says. "That person was Dr. Joynt. He and Mrs. Joynt were very welcoming and supportive," he said. "Bob recommended I stay in Rochester after my residency." Honch did, building an outstanding career at RGH. His experience was mirrored by many of the residents whose time at Rochester was enriched by knowing the remarkable Dr. Bob.

ᴈ❧   ᴈ❧   ᴈ❧

Teaching young people how to become skilled doctors is a proud calling. And finding, recruiting, and supporting great teachers is key to the success of an academic medical center and for building a world-class neurology department. A department chair needs physicians and medical scientists who are both secure in their expertise and endowed with the gift to inspire others. At finding and retaining such people, Dr. Bob was a master.

Dr. Bob, of course, was himself a superb educator. He relished being with students—and they with him. Joe Martin recalls those days in the late '60s: "During my two years at Rochester I attended neurology rounds regularly to watch Bob in his extraordinary capacity as a 'neurological wise man.' At grand rounds, he was always the star. He had an amazingly broad breadth of neurological interests." He also had a way of personalizing a subject, showing how our neurological patterning helps create the people we become.

One of Dr. Bob's first moves was to develop the neurology residency program, then and now one of the department's "jewels." He chose David Marsh, a Scottish-trained Englishman, as its first director, a post held in following years by Roger Kurlan and more recently by Ralph Jozefowicz. It's hardly an overstatement to say that, around the world, hundreds of neurologists and neuroscientists recognize the importance of what they learned during their years of training in Rochester.

UR's neurology residents have always been a stellar group. The first two were Donald Castle, who came to Rochester from Iowa with Dr. Bob, and Marvin Goldstein. Soon joining them were Robert ("Berch") Griggs, who would succeed Dr. Joynt as chair; Alexander Reeves, soon to become chair of neurology at Dartmouth; Richard Moxley, who helped develop an internationally acclaimed neuromuscular unit; and Ira Shoulson, who brought Rochester to international fame for studies of movement disorders.

"As father of our department, Bob Joynt set the tone," says Ralph Jozefowicz, who himself has an international reputation as an inspiring teacher. "Now, as director of neurology's residency program, what I look for in a student is what Bob valued: integrity, loyalty, and humility. Integrity is being honest when no one is looking, loyalty means you are there for each other, and humility means it's not all about you." Recalling his mentor, Dr. Jozefowicz says, "It was Bob who got me interested in teaching when I was a resident. He asked me to give a lecture to the neuro staff. I got up there and almost had a panic attack. I thought, I can't sit down, I just have to get through this. By the next year, I discovered I *wanted* to teach—and Bob found the money to fund me. We still train residents to teach the medical students, and Bob started, supported, and inspired that."

For many of those early residents, memories of their classroom days with Dr. Bob are unforgettable. Barney Stern, professor of neurology at the University of Maryland and director of its residency program, was one of those residents. "Training under Bob was an absolutely unique experience," he says. "Even though we knew a VIP neurologist was coming into the room, he would put us at ease in seconds. Often he would elicit physical findings in a patient that we residents would never have discovered. He had an uncanny ability to listen to our presentations, assessments, and opinions and make us feel we were having a discussion with a friend, not 'the Chairman,' who also happened to be a world-class individual."

Richard Nordgren, an award-winning professor at Dartmouth University's medical school, remembers the beginning of his six years of training in Rochester with pleasure, for both its scholarly nature and its conviviality. The neurology residency program was just beginning at that time, but Nordgren soon found himself part of a congenial group of trainees and faculty who, on occasion, would expand journal club meetings at Dr. Bob's home to the downstairs poker table.

A quiet, unassuming manner was the quintessential Bob Joynt—and it was evident to all who met him. Barney Stern once asked Dr. Bob for a letter of recommendation at a time when he was applying for a position at Johns Hopkins. He still treasures a copy of the somewhat unusual letter that Bob supplied: "Dear Dr. McKhann, Barney Stern is a good guy. I suggest you hire him. Best regards, Bob Joynt." McKhann did—and Stern became a man of consequence among American neurologists.

~ ~ ~

Medical scientists are key to building a strong department. Some search for better ways to treat patients, others focus on "bench research"—pure science, which in neurology means exploring the complex partnership between the brain and the body.

One key to the new department's success would be attracting the "best of the best" to join the Joynt team of scientific investigators. A researcher himself, Dr. Bob built strong relationships with neuroscientists at other institutions. Many were eager to work collaboratively with the UR scientists on projects of mutual interest. Others, like Richard Moxley, Guy Molinari, and Celia Sladek, moved to Rochester to join the Joynt team. Some of the best, like Berch Griggs and Ira Shoulson, had been trained right here, graduates of the Department of Neurology's outstanding residency training program.

"Bob had the ability to recognize good work in clinical science," says the senior faculty member Richard Moxley. "He also had the ability to network with people who were doing good work, synthesize what they had to offer, and use that information to nurture those of us working in various kinds of science. I think Bob's real contribution was that he was focused less on a specific area of science and more on the big, ongoing challenge of how to build the fabric of science."

Dr. Bob also had a gift for attracting research funding from both federal and private sources (including the UR's first million-dollar federal grant for Alzheimer's research). For medical scientists, this was compelling reason to come to Rochester—or to stay here after their residencies. One of them was Berch Griggs. "Bob had an NIH training grant that enabled him to support a laboratory and faculty stipends. Bob had two technicians working for Adolf Weindl, a German scientist who was on faculty here. Weindl and Bob published very good papers, some of Bob's most authoritative work. As chief resident, I also had two technicians funded with Bob's support. This, for the time, was highly unusual. Using Bob's lab and what I had learned at NIH, I set up the first proper muscle biopsy lab in western New York."

The new chairman may have been a rainmaker for his researchers, but he was far more than that. As a neuroscientist himself, he made it a point to support and encourage his researchers; he knew firsthand how long and difficult is the search for answers to science's big questions. That supportive attitude impressed Moxley, a newcomer to Rochester in 1974 from Johns Hopkins. Bob spoke with a senior professor, asking him to work with the young man. "Then, as a kind of christening, Bob asked me to run the nerve conduction lab," Moxley recalls. "I can tell you it's very motivating to have the blessing of someone like Bob, who was such a strong believer in the team approach. It ups the ante. Two really committed, intelligent, collegial people trying to solve the same problem almost always stand a better chance of succeeding than one person working alone."

Often, the chairman would partner with a basic science researcher. One of these was Celia Sladek, PhD, now a professor at the University of Colorado. "Dr. Joynt was eager to get grants that would have both a basic science component and a clinical component," she says. Bob helped Sladek develop a research program targeting the hormones vasopressin and oxytocin. Since both hormones are regulated by the hypothalamus, Dr. Bob's own early interest, Sladek had the good fortune to have the department chair as her research partner, whenever his time permitted. Sladek and

Joynt collaborated on five articles published in medical journals on osmotic control of vasopressin.

Ira Shoulson, a University of Rochester MD who would put the university on the international map for his work in experimental therapeutics for Parkinson's disease, Huntington's disease, and other movement disorders, and now a professor of neurology at Georgetown University, also found the chairman to be a strong supporter. "Bob was always interested in therapeutics, even at a time when that was not prominent in neurology. He was an incredibly strong leader, in large part because he understood where he was going. He was criticized by some for not being more authoritarian, but he was very productive. His accomplishments in academia are rich, eclectic, and enduring."

Bob Joynt was indeed productive. The astonishing fact is that during his twenty-two years as chair, his name appeared on more than eighty scientific papers, as "first author" on thirty-two of them, on topics ranging from vision problems, memory loss, stroke, senility, epilepsy, Alzheimer's, various endocrine studies, to (foresightedly) the possibility of neural transplants.

It seems that everyone who interacted with Bob learned something from him—sometimes about science, sometimes about life itself. Because his personality was so well integrated, many people saw both sides at the same time. Berch Griggs was one: "When I arrived from NIH, Bob asked me to be his chief resident. He was a master clinician and a magnet for interesting cases, and a lot of my early papers were based on patients he'd sent me. He was very wise—and he knew *everybody*. Everyone was important to Bob. That's the thing that is impressive. It's hard not to sort people into 'important' and 'not important.' Bob never did that. He enjoyed weekly lunches with his secretaries, and he knew the names of all the people who cleaned the offices." For Bob Joynt, everyone had value.

It's true—sometimes it takes more than tough, upfront leadership qualities to succeed. Dr. Joynt's longtime assistant Nancy Baldwin credits other, softer aspects as key to why her boss was so successful: "He was a very kind and gentle person. He gave you a job to do, expected you to do it, and let you have free range in completing the job," she says. "He surrounded himself with people he trusted and let them do their job."

∾　∾　∾

In 1985, Dr. Robert J. Joynt became the fourth Dean of the School of Medicine and Dentistry, an appointment that would see him leave the department he had founded, nourished, and cherished for twenty-two years. How well did Dr. Bob succeed in filling his early promise to build the best Department of Neurology in the country? Certainly the department's rise to national prominence under his leadership—in the three traditional measurements for academic medical centers: the quality of clinical care, teaching, and research—is self-evident.

But University of Maryland's Barney Stern, who knows the territory well, has another answer to that question:

> I know some will measure success by counting patient visits and clinical dollars. Others will sum up NIH research funds. I offer another measure. In 1980, we began to have a reunion of Rochester-trained neurologists at the annual meeting of the American Academy of Neurology. There were only a few at that first gathering.
>
> Now, every year, there are dozens of us, spanning several generations of faculty and trainees, representing every region of the country and many international locales. Awards are given, and a bit of fund-raising takes place. But most important, there are hugs and catching-up, remembrances, and storytelling. And it all goes back to Bob and his vision. I submit to you that this may be the most meaningful metric of them all.

THE COMIC SPIRIT
(AND HOW HE WIELDED IT)

"Margaret, I hope I won't be remembered for just being funny."
—Dr. Bob, home again at last, after
yet another after-dinner talk

How poignant is that wistful plea! We've seen how throughout his life Dr. Bob was operating on a very high level in multiple fields, often simultaneously—as scientist, compassionate physician, renowned professor, editor, dean, vice president, mentor, treasured friend, beloved husband and father. Bob Joynt's reputation always was solid gold.

Yet mention his name and often the response is something like this: "Oh, what a wonderful man! He was *so* funny!" Of *course* he was, he couldn't help but be funny. He was smart as a whip, his memory was prodigious, and, above all, he was Irish. Never the kind of "wise guy" who leaves them rolling in the aisles, Bob Joynt's bred-in-the-bone humor left people feeling better about life, cleansed by laughter.

"I have a sense there was a single core, a profound unity in which the person and the professional were bound together with humor," says his good friend and former UR president Dennis O'Brien. "He knew himself, he knew his work, he knew humanity—and humor ran through the whole story."

"Bob reminds me of the great American humorist Will Rogers," says Seymour Schwartz, the Medical Center's former chair of surgery. "His humor was unsophisticated, never mean-spirited or unkind, and very, very funny. I once asked Bob to give the after-dinner speech for 120 chiefs of surgery who had come to Rochester from universities across the country, and a few from around the world. Before long, not only were all the guests laughing, but I saw many of them taking notes." That evening Bob told the distinguished surgeons: "The most important quality a dean must have is absolute integrity. [Pregnant pause.] Once you've learned to fake *that . . .* !"

In all his interactions—with students, residents, faculty, staff, friends, and colleagues—Bob Joynt could make the social fabric of the occasion stronger and smoother by judiciously wielding that irresistible weapon, his remarkable, witty humor.

🐚   🐚   🐚

Comedy's duty, said the great French playwright Molière, is to correct men by amusing them. Let it never be said that Dr. Bob's chief aim in life was to be a corrector. Yet as his colleague and good friend the late David Goldblatt, MD, once wrote, "Bob likes to give advice." That advice almost always came with a comic twist, as in Dr. Bob's famous Tenth Commandment for interns: "Spend what time you can with your family. During my house officer training, my wife and I made it a point to go out at least two times a week. . . . I would go out on Tuesdays and she would go out on Fridays." That's a perfect example of comedian Sid Caesar's first rule of comedy: "Base it on truth, and put a curlicue on the end."

The comic spirit was so deeply integral to the Joynt persona that, while we were laughing, we might miss how he was using humor for serious purposes. Ira Shoulson explains: "Bob's humor was an essential element of engagement that helped develop relationships and forge compromise—vital attributes for a department chair and dean [and later CEO]."

"Berch" Griggs, who succeeded Dr. Bob as chair of neurology, tells this story of how the famous Joynt sense of humor could be put to important work. "We had an NIH group coming up from Washington who could give us a much-needed grant. As the new department chair, I was exceedingly nervous about this meeting, not helped at all by the fact that the visitors all seemed very stiff and formal. Then Bob, as the new dean, walked into the room, holding five crisp, one-dollar bills. Greeting the group warmly, he parceled out the bills, handing one to each of the five men. Puzzled for a moment, they suddenly got the joke—and all broke up in laughter, as did Bob and I." This funny mocking of illegal "payola" practices worked. "The site visitors all were impressed with the department's work—and we got the grant," said Griggs.

As Dr. Bob slipped those new dollar bills into his wallet, was he recalling Aristotle's advice? "The secret of humor is to surprise," said the sage of Athens. Paul Griner, the former CEO of Strong Memorial Hospital, often saw Dr. Bob use the surprise factor to win over a wary audience. He's never forgotten the new chair of neurology's first presentation at an internal medicine grand rounds, when this stranger from Iowa was about to be judged by a competitive group of colleagues, a packed house from a different specialty, Griner's own. What profundity, what depth of vision would the new man offer? Here's what they heard: "I've always thought that internists don't know much about neurology. I believed that most of you think that a 'Babinski'[1] is a Polish martini." The group exploded with laughter, Griner recalls, and everyone relaxed.

⚘　⚘　⚘

Comedy can cut. Humor can heal. In a top-tier medical center, where tension almost always runs high, having someone like Dr. Bob working at the highest levels of administration was therapeutic. Peter Robinson, current UR vice president and COO of the Medical Center, worked closely with Dr. Bob during the often-trying days of the early 1990s. "Everyone knew about Bob's humor," Robinson has said. "Not everyone knew how he could use that humor to set up an environment where you could deal with tough issues in a relaxed environment. He had a very beguiling and intelligent way of going about problem-solving."

Former UR president Dennis O'Brien adds this: "If you came to a meeting in a controversial mode, you were immediately going to be *enveloped*. Bob was simply not going to react to your antagonism. Always, for him, there was a larger dimension to be considered."

⚘　⚘　⚘

What upped the ante on a Bob Joynt story was the way he told it, slipping the comic surprise in quietly, at just the right moment, his timing perfect . . . and, as laughter broke out, following up with a little Irish half smile. Ira Shoulson reminds us, "Few are born and die with a twinkle in the eye—the occulofacial sparkle that Bob enjoyed. His wit was quick, clean, and thought-provoking, and the delivery smooth and captivating."

Bob's control over his material was absolute; he also was comfortable in his own skin. As a result, he could afford to be daring (as he was with the site visitors from Washington). Marshall Lichtman recalls a memorable commencement when Dean Joynt stepped up to the podium to greet an entering class of eager medical students who just had been welcomed formally by the university president. Now the dean stood before them, the man who would help guide their lives for the next four years. All expected words of wisdom. "Greetings to you and welcome," said Dean Bob. "I hope you all had a good summer. . . . As for myself, I had a root canal." He then began riffing on the topic in a manner that can only be called hilarious. "No other dean anywhere in America would consider beginning a speech by talking about his root canal," says Lichtman, shaking his head and smiling, as he recalls the incident. The words of wisdom, of course, came soon after, delivered to an audience that Dean Joynt now owned.

Root canals and wisdom, two unlikely partners, woven together in a fifteen-minute welcoming speech. This sounds like what Christopher Morley, a favorite author of Dr. Bob's, had in mind when he wrote: "Humor is perhaps a sense of intellectual perspective: an awareness that some things are really important, others not; and that the two are most oddly jumbled in everyday affairs."

⁂ ⁂ ⁂

Dr. Bob was "undoubtedly the most sought-after dinner speaker our specialty has known," recalled David Golblatt. "Bob's sense of humor made him the consummate toastmaster, after-dinner speaker, and visiting professor," remarked Berch Griggs. "He could make a tense meeting with department chairs, anxious faculty, or site visitors dissolve into gales of laughter." Older members of the neurology faculty recall a certain departmental budget meeting. Tension was high as they settled into their seats. Where would the cuts come? Suddenly Chairman Bob wheeled in a full-size human skeleton, requisitioned for the occasion from anatomy. There was a burst of laughter, along with recognition that whereas the budget might be "bare bones," the department itself was healthy.

Sometimes just plain fun was in order. Seasonally, out came the Santa Claus suit, the leprechaun hat, the green beer at home on St. Patrick's day—even the rubber replica of the cerebral cortex worn as headgear. *That,* used judiciously, could be counted on to enliven otherwise decorous departmental meetings.

The fact is, life's comical aspects often cannot be overlooked. (Someone always slips on the banana peel.) Dr. Joe Martin recalls, "At graduation exercises one year, we had a trustee who was known to have a fondness for the bottle. The day was warm, and just before we began to process, she keeled over. Bob, of course, rushed to her side. When he returned I asked what was wrong. 'The Irish flu,' he said, soberly. I got the point."

Perhaps, in the end, it was at the personal level that Dr. Bob's humor could be the most beneficent. Ray Mayewski recalls that "as young faculty, his humor helped us deal with issues that were new to us—how our work with patients related to our role in the hospital and as teachers in the classroom." With his wise counsel came a reminder, often the homespun truth with which he is most closely identified: "You can't always be right. But you can always be kind. . . . Remember, there is no limit to kindness."

For that, Dr. Bob himself was a near-perfect example.

A Few of the Famed "Joyntisms"

They enriched his conversation like plums in a plum pudding. Dr. Bob's favorite aphorisms were wise, funny, and applicable to the whole human comedy. But as Dennis O'Brien points out: "Bob did not use humor as a social Band-Aid. His was humor appropriate to the situation and from heart to heart, whether to the student, colleague, patient, or friend." Enjoy!

- "Even a blind pig gets an acorn sometime, but not without sticking his nose in the mud and rooting around."
- "I wouldn't have seen it if I hadn't believed it." (A cautionary for scientists.)
- "The only thing harder than being a saint is living with one."
- "If you're going to teach a dog a new trick, be sure you know more than the dog."

- "The problem with trouble is that it usually starts out as fun."
- "To a man with a big hammer, every small problem looks like a nail."
- "The number of lacunae in the brain is equal to the number of gravy stains on a man's tie."
- "There are two kinds of headaches: those relieved by aspirin and those you refer to your friends."
- "A man is in trouble when the volume of his lateral ventricles exceeds the volume of the lobes of his prostate."
- "Beware of women in large hats" (borrowed from his own UI mentor, Dr. Adolph Sahs).
- "Even a broken clock is right twice a day."
- "Bad apples fall close to the tree."
- "Give the patient time and he or she will tell you what the problem is."
- "If you have two dollars to spend, spend one on bread and the other on a rose."

9

DEAN BOB'S TEN COMMANDMENTS
FOR INTERNS

During his years as Dean of the School of Medicine and Dentistry, Dr. Bob fostered warm relationships with medical students, residents, and interns. He loved being in their company, relished their fresh ideas, and enjoyed joking with them. Above all, he wanted to help them grow, not just in their chosen profession but also as human beings.

Dr. Bob knew the value of mentoring, as he had been mentored by A. H. Sahs and others at the University of Iowa. And he knew the importance of striving for a balanced life, even during the stressful years of rigorous medical training. The year after he became chair of the new Department of Neurology, he was asked to address the university's graduating medical students. He gave the young doctors sage advice that day, and was invited to repeat his Ten Commandments on many other occasions. A host of UR Medical Center graduates remember them well.

Ten Commandments for a Successful Internship

#1. Listen! Your patient is trying to tell you something.

"If you have thirty minutes with the patient, spend twenty-nine minutes talking to him, one minute with the examination, and no minutes with the laboratory findings. You will then have apportioned your time correctly.

"If you can read a journal article or see a patient, see a patient—you will learn more. The internship is perhaps the greatest educational experience devised by man, a time to interview, examine, and take care of patients, lots of them. There is no better text. It does little good to know all about the antibodies to colonic carcinoma if you haven't done a rectal examination."

#2. *The Rule of the Garden Sparrow and the Golden Eagle*

"You will see a thousand pneumonias for one lupus erythematosus. Don't try to be a hero with the esoteric diagnosis. Obscure diagnoses will only cost the patient time and money. When you hear hoof beats, don't think of zebras."

#3. *Hark the Words of a Seventeenth-Century Monk*

"William of Occam (Ockham) is credited with saying, *Etia non sunt multipliana necessitatem.* This was later described as the Law of Parsimony, or Logical Frugality, popularly known as Occam's Razor. It means, don't make two diagnoses when one will do. An intern's life is complicated enough without your working overtime at it."

#4. *The Rule of Pogo[1]*

"Pogo said, 'We have met the enemy and he is us.' So call for help when you are in trouble. It is the patient who is important, not your ego."

#5. *Don't Fool with Mother Nature*

"God protects fools and interns. When a patient is doing well, don't intervene with new medicines or new tests. Many have made their reputations by knowing when to do nothing."

#6. *Alexander Graham Bell, You Done Us Wrong![2]*

"The telephone is neither a stethoscope nor a reflex hammer. You can't palpate an abdomen by long distance. Let the consultant make a fool of himself by not seeing his patient when he is called. You get up and see the patient. (You probably don't need all that sleep anyway.)"

#7. *Don't Be Dun In by Bradstreet.*

"Drug companies have a good financial rating because patients and doctors use too many drugs. Many home medicine cabinets [are examples of this]. Many women's pocketbooks are traveling drugstores—the only thing they don't hold is the soda fountain. We ought to have two textbooks of medicine, one to tell us how to treat patients, the other to tell us how to treat the patient after the complications of treatment set in. Use drugs judiciously and sparingly. You do most patients a greater service by eliminating, not adding more, medications."

#8. *We Are All Biodegradable*

"We all have to die sometime. People die even in a university hospital with an excellent teaching service. Immortality used to be awarded by the historian; now it seems to be the prerogative of the intensive care unit physician. It is not a crime to die with the sodium 5 mEq off normal. It is rarely difficult to decide when your efforts at prolonging life are no longer possible or charitable. It is usually the exercise of good common sense."

#9. *Emily Post,[3] Where Are You When We Really Need You!*

"Don't forget your manners. Internship is a time when you become tired and impatient and sometimes forget the niceties. However, when I am waiting for that Great Neurologist in the sky, I don't want to be addressed as 'Pop' or 'Dad' by a boorish house officer. Also, I don't want my case history, bowel movements, and vital signs bruited around the lunchroom. Many patients have little left but their dignity. You preserve that!"

#10. *Keep the Home Fires Burning*

"Internship is a hard time, one of the hardest you will experience. It's just as hard or harder on the spouse and family. Few of us attain fame in our lives, so the legacies we leave are in our families. Spend what time you have available with them." And the famous Bob punch line: "During my house officer training, my wife and I made a point to go out for dinner away from the children at least two times a week. I would go out on Tuesdays; she would go out on Fridays."

DR. BOB, EDITOR EXTRAORDINAIRE

*"Even editors had a patron saint, I've learned. It was St. John, the
Apostle. As it turned out, unfortunately, John was thrown into a
pot of boiling oil for his efforts. I am certain that this action may
find approval among many authors. St. John survived, however.
In the end, you see, the editor always wins."*

—Dr. Robert Joynt (1999)

It was inevitable, of course, that his voracious appetite for the
written word would lead our Dr. Bob into a secondary—and parallel—career as an influential editor. During the 1980s, his hand
would guide two neurology journals (as editor in chief of *Archives of
Neurology,* now *JAMA-Neurology,* and founding editor of *Seminars in
Neurology*) as well as a major neurology textbook.

Let's call the decades of the '60s and '70s Dr. Bob's training
ground for the work that came later. During those years, he was
appointed consecutively to the editorial boards of *Medical Digest,
Cortex, Neurology, Brain and Language,* and *Perspectives in Biology and
Medicine.* During editorial board meetings he absorbed the gener-
ally accepted parameters of what constitutes a good medical journal:
accurate reporting of sound science, articles relevant to health care
and health policy, and—not least—content that will interest readers.

The editor's job is not an easy one. It is naive to believe that
scientific inquiry is always conducted on a rarefied plane free of
economic and political perspectives. As a result, the editor's own
character and judgment should be strong and beyond reproach.
Only then can the journal that he or she represents be truly independent, buttressed against powerful outside interests.

For authors, timing of publication always will be of primary
importance. Who tells the story first—about a promising new drug

study, a clinical review of a new device—can mean professional advancement for the author(s), grant money for the department involved, profits for a drug company. The editor, on the other hand, must resist pressures to publish prematurely. Is the science sound? Are the reviewers qualified to judge the study's methods and results? It was during these decades that Dr. Bob learned how to deal with both issues and authors, honing the skills required to be an effective editor.

Lucretia McClure, the longtime head of the Edward G. Miner Medical Library at the University of Rochester, points out that editor Bob came to the job of medical editing with one big advantage: his ability to stay calm amidst a storm of personalities and to defuse anger with humor. These were tools he would need as he entered an arena not immune from common stresses that result from competing egos, jealousy, and academic pressures to publish.

At the heart of the issue, of course, is Dr. Bob's love of language, his breadth of knowledge, and his skill in asking the right questions: Who are the best people to review this material? Is it timely? Will it interest our readers?

❧   ❧   ❧

What made Dr. Bob a good editor? Here's what his longtime colleague Vladimir Hachinski has to say about that. Dr. Hachinski was the editor of *Stroke*, the past president of the World Federation of Neurology, and the 2014 Brain Scholar at Cambridge, Oxford, and London Universities. "Bob had the talent to spot talent—and encourage and enable that talent to be put into practice," says Hachinski. "My association with *Archives of Neurology* goes back to its founding days with Maurice Van Allen in Iowa. I was just a boy then. When Bob became editor, he asked me to stay on the editorial board. But when he suggested I create a section called 'Controversies in Neurology,' I said, 'Are you sure? I think I'm still too young to take this on.' Bob said, 'You'll do fine.'" And Hachinski did.

"Controversies" became the section that residents often read first, and it became a valuable teaching tool. On one occasion, the column raised a storm of controversy. The controversy addressed was: Should magnesium sulphate be used to treat eclampsia? Hachinski concluded that the drug should be used only in the laboratory, for clinical trials, and "for history." When a threatening letter arrived from the American College of Obstetrics and Gynecology—"Why should a Canadian be telling us what to do?"—Dr. Bob was reassuring. "Don't worry, Vlad, we'll support you. Nothing will happen." Nothing did happen. But supporting people, whether family, students, faculty, or friends, was what Bob Joynt was all about.

❧ ❧ ❧

More needs to be said about *Archives of Neurology*, perhaps editor Bob's best-loved editorial challenge. Dr. Bob became chief editor of the monthly journal of peer-reviewed articles on neurological diseases and their treatment in 1982 and remained its editor for the next fifteen years. A closer look reveals how much has changed in medical publishing over the past thirty years.

The invitation for Dr. Bob to take on the editorship came from *JAMA's* editor in chief George Lundberg. This would be a professional plum indeed; it was also a major undertaking for an already busy physician and academician. Having accepted the offer during the summer of '82, Dr. Bob and Margaret were once again on the road, heading to Iowa City to gather up the contents of the *Archives* office at the University of Iowa. Waiting for them was a trunkload of manuscripts, all the records kept by the former editor Maurice Van Allen, his wife, Janet, and Janet's big book of US postal stamps of varying values used for *Archives* mailings. The trip was a sociable one—the Van Allens and the Joynts were good friends. With the car loaded up and farewells exchanged, our indefatigable pair was once again back on the road, but not to Rochester.

For the next six weeks, the Joynts and the *Archives* material resided in Princeton, where Dr. Bob had a grant to study American public-health policy. Weekday mornings were spent in class, afternoons were devoted to poring over the journal's manuscripts, whose authors were eagerly waiting for a response from the new editor. Margaret, who had written a paper in Cambridge on the rights of women who married a foreign national, spent the hot summer days reading through the collection of books by women authors in the air-conditioned Princeton library.

That September back in Pittsford, editor Bob expanded his office in the basement of the Joynt family home on Sandpiper

Lane. Let's look back thirty years and step down into that subterranean room where an early issue of *Archives* is being prepared. The publication center is spartan, amusingly archaic by today's standards: two long tables, a single phone, two typewriters, a copy machine, stacks of paper, a pile of envelopes, a giant roll of stamps, and later a useful postage meter. It's five o'clock on a summer afternoon and the full staff is here: editor in chief Dr. Bob (who has been at the UR Medical Center since 7 a.m.) and his editorial assistant, eldest daughter "Trish," along with summer help, youngest daughter Kathy.

That fall, a flood of manuscripts begins arriving at the *Archives* mailbox at the University of Rochester. Their arrival initiates a chain of events on Sandpiper Lane that now, three decades later, seems quaint. The copy machine in the basement grumbles almost daily as it churns out multiples of each manuscript, followed by dozens of review sheets, and acceptance/rejection letters. The phone line is kept busy with conversations with reviewers and discussions with *JAMA* staff in Chicago. Stacks of manila envelopes have to be stuffed with review copies, run through the postage meter, and mailed to selected neurologist reviewers at universities across the country. Authors have to be sent the news, whether good or disappointing.

Like many beginnings, it was simple, but it worked. In fact, it worked so well that *Archives in Neurology* grew in size and importance. An unusual later addition to the basement office—a trunk-size computer—hinted that a new age was on the way. Foreseeing the future, editor Bob urged George Lundberg, *JAMA's* editor in chief, to adopt the next iteration of the revolutionary technology. As a result, *Archives* was the first of *JAMA's* specialty journals to use computers in the publication process. In 1987, the *Archives* operation moved to the University of Rochester, with Bob continuing as editor for fifteen years, signing off in 1996.

∾   ∾   ∾

The "editing bug" apparently had bitten deep. At an American Academy of Neurology annual meeting in 1982, Dr. Bob was called aside by A. B. Baker, the author of neurology's chief textbook, *Clinical Neurology*, and one of the four Midwestern founders of the Academy. "Bob, I want you to take over the editorship," Dr. Baker said. "Think about it during this meeting and let me know." The answer: "Yes. Of course!"

Abe Baker put his faith in Bob as the one to carry on the leadership of what had been long regarded as the most comprehensive neurology textbook for students, residents, and practicing neurologists. Bob's many national connections and leadership helped boost sales for the book, which was published in loose-leaf form so it could be easily updated. The neurologist Berch Griggs, later the book's coeditor, says, "We worked to update the chapters every three years, adding new sections as neurology itself was rapidly expanding."

Eventually, the arrival of on-line publishing brought an end to the once-essential textbook, although its life was extended briefly using a CD format. Neither of its editors needed the work. Bob was busy as dean of the medical school and chief editor of *Archives of Neurology*. Griggs, Bob's successor as chair of the Department of Neurology, subsequently became the new editor of *Neurology*. "Bob was sad to see [the long-running series and its annual edition] disappear," says Griggs, "and most of its authors and many of the readers lamented its demise."

Another editorial opportunity already had appeared, however. In 1985, a publisher asked editor Bob to create a medical journal with a new format. The concept: each issue would focus on a single clinical problem, such as epilepsy or muscular dystrophy. Bob agreed, and *Seminars in Neurology* came to life, continuing today as an on-line journal. A guest editor prepares each issue, recruiting other specialists to report on trends in diagnosing, evaluating, and treating the neurological condition being featured.

During these years Bob wore multiple editorial hats as he was appointed consecutively to the editorial boards of *Medical Digest, Cortex, Neurology* (the journal of the American Academy of Neurology), *Brain and Language,* and *Perspectives in Biology and Medicine.* It's clear he knew well the rigors and responsibilities that come with the job. Here is the full text of the congratulatory note he sent to a neurologist friend in Baltimore: "I have just been apprised of the fact that you have accepted the position as an editor of ____. Are you out of your mind? Go full speed ahead. Bob."

❧   ❧   ❧

Dr. Bob's work on the *Archives of Neurology* and the Baker-Joynt textbook was interrupted in 1993 by a serious illness that incapacitated him for several months. At that time, the late David Goldblatt, *Archives'* associate editor, stepped into the chief editor role.

Of all Dr. Bob's editorships, *Archives of Neurology* was his best loved, according to daughter Kathy, his early assistant and now managing editor of *Neurology*. Kathy was in his hospital room at Strong Memorial Hospital when Dr. Bob was struggling up from a months-long coma. As her father slowly recognized her, he made his first attempt at voicing a word. Still not fully articulated, the word fragment was "Arch . . ."

In 1998, Berch Griggs, by then editor of *Neurology*, asked him to become section editor of a newsletter within that journal, the most widely read and heavily cited in its field. Bob named the section "Changes + People + Comments." "Changes" discussed new developments in neurology and "People" included an interview with a neurologist making a difference in the specialty. "Comments" gave editor Bob an opportunity to both editorialize and amuse readers familiar with his wry and witty off-hand style. One of those comments suggests that he knew well the rigors related to journal editing:

> I once asked a well-known editor: What are the requirements for the job? Without hesitation, he answered, "It's good to have a working knowledge of the English language, but it is absolutely necessary that you have a vindictive streak in your soul." And then there is a story of the editor who died and met St. Peter at the Pearly Gates. St. Peter asked, "What did you do [in life]?" The applicant answered, "I was an editor." St. Peter said, "Come right on in. You have had your hell on earth."

৵   ৵   ৵

Since editor Bob's time, the world of medical science has changed exponentially, and with it, the role of the medical editor. UR's Robert Gross, editor in chief of *Neurology*, explains some of those changes: "Submitted manuscripts today receive much harsher scrutiny than when Bob was editing. We have rules we must follow and checklists that must be filled out. Each clinical trial under review must have been registered on clinicaltrials.gov before we'll look at it. Standards of transparency now are very high. In the past, articles submitted by pharmaceutical companies often were prepared by ghostwriters. Now the names of *all* writers must be listed in the journal."

Timing of publication is even more important today, according to Dr. Gross. "It used to be that if a one-year clinical trial of a drug showed positive results at six months, the data would be published prematurely—as in the case of Vioxx—only to be found inaccurate at the end of the twelve-month testing period originally scheduled."

Yes, things change. But in no way does the current culture of publishing diminish what Bob Joynt achieved during his years as editor. As Dr. Gross points out, "The role of editor years ago was much more all-encompassing than it is now. Today we are heavily constrained by checks, rules, and regulations, all designed to improve the quality of reporting. Back then, if an editor thought something was OK, it was OK." That's why it was (and still is) important to choose an editor with all the necessary attributes: good judgment, language skills, networking knowledge, sound science, a capacity for hard work, and the ability to steer the ship through stormy weather. In other words, someone just like editor Bob.

ONWARD AND UPWARD, DR. BOB!

1966–84

During the early '60s, as the fledgling Department of Neurology flourished, so did the reputation of the "rookie from Iowa" who was at its helm, inspiring and guiding the growth of the department and supporting its faculty. In retrospect, what we see is a powerful parallel trajectory.

Scarcely a decade after his arrival, "Bob Joynt in Rochester" had become the go-to guy for colleagues across the country who needed an audience-engaging, articulate spokesman for a current topic relating to neurology, medical education, public health— or one of the highly amusing after-dinner talks for which he was becoming well known. Whenever Dr. Bob was on the podium, the audience was sure to hear a thoroughly informed talk based on sound science, and could leave the auditorium with a smile, chuckle, or guffaw. No small benefit to those whose métier deeply involves them with human pain and suffering.

Dr. Bob's disarming, witty approach to serious topics was a guaranteed crowd pleaser. As a result, during the following decades his calendar was full of speaking engagements. From 1966 to 1984, the years of his chairmanship, he lectured at universities in New York, Colorado, Minnesota, Tennessee, Iowa, Louisiana, Maryland, Texas, Virginia, Kansas, Pennsylvania, Nebraska, San Francisco, and overseas in England, Germany, and Lebanon—often speaking more than once at several of these institutions, and often to receive a citation.

❧   ❧   ❧

People liked to be with Dr. Bob. But the wit, charm, and kindly nature were a cover for his deep seriousness and extraordinary capacity for hard work. As a result, his ascent within the profession was meteoric. In a rare triple play, Dr. Bob would chair all of neurology's "big three" professional organizations: the American Academy of Neurology (1977–79), the American Board of Psychiatry and Neurology (1979), and the American Neurological Association (1987–88). He would become editor in chief of two major journals and an important textbook, and he would sit on many other editorial boards. In addition, during his years as department chair, he was a member of eighteen scientific organizations, rising in several of them from committee ranks to key leadership roles. Many of these societies had a special focus, such as epilepsy, electroencephalography, experimental biology and medicine, Alzheimer's disease, psychiatry, brain research, and the history of medicine. All were of interest to the new chair of neurology.

Could Dr. Bob have been more involved? Yes, of course—and he was. During these same years, he was a medical consultant, chairman, or committee member of twenty federal, national, and international groups targeting such disparate (but medically related) topics as research grant requests, EEG certification, residency reviews, as well as research on communicable diseases such as influenza and Guillain-Barre syndrome, neuroepidemiology, Huntington's disease, amyotrophic lateral sclerosis (ALS), multiple sclerosis, Alzheimer's disease, aging research, dyslexia, and cerebral survival.

The networks that Dr. Bob was building among the growing number of neurologists at academic medical centers across the country did much to enhance his national reputation and that of the department and the university, as did his growing editorial work. Nor was it just in America that he was becoming well known. As early as his faculty days at UI, his interest in aphasia (the loss of ability to use words) had linked him with a quartet of European scientists with the same interest; the five men quickly became good friends, as did their wives. Later, Dr. Bob's contact with the World Federation of Neurologists expanded his professional networks—and his workload.

What made all this extraordinary effort possible was Dr. Bob's tenacity of purpose—and his early decision at the University of Rochester "to hire people smarter than I am—and then get out of their way." Never a micromanager, his efforts always were for the greater good, never for enhancing his own ego.

The distinguished scientist Ira Shoulson, an early Joynt recruit, has a simple explanation of what made Bob tick and his efforts so selfless: "[Bob] honed self-effacement to a high art. . . . [Instead,] he busied himself in advancing neurology as a scientific, clinical, and therapeutic force in modern medicine." What could be a grander calling?

Bob at age two. Circa 1927.

Bob at age three. Circa 1928.

Bob with sisters. *Left to right:* Peggy, Mary Ellen, Bob, Patty. Circa 1926.

Junior high boy scouts: Bob (*second row, second from right*). Circa 1938.

Le Mars High School football team, 1943. *First row, third from right:* Robert Joynt (#78); *second row, third from left*, Warren Stamp (#77), former chairman, Department of Orthopedics, University of Virginia; *second row, far right*, Coach Carey; *third row, second from left*, Tom Starzl, pioneer in kidney and liver transplants.

Sergeant Joynt in India during World War II.

Bob's father, Robert J. Joynt.

Bob's mother, Mayme (nee Teefey) Joynt.

Bob's paternal grandmother (*first row, second from left*) and grandfather (*first row, center*) with nine children; Bob's father (*second row, third from left*). Circa 1905.

Bob's maternal grandfather, Patrick Teefey.

Bob's maternal grandmother, Nell (nee O'Connor) Teefey.

Ancestral cabin in Shanaglish, near Gort in County Galway, Ireland.

Bob and Margaret, 1951.

Bob at University of Iowa Medical School graduation, 1952.

Wedding, Bob and Margaret, 1953.

Bob's family in Le Mars, 1955.

Department of Neurology, University of Iowa College of Medicine, 1960. *Left to right:* Arthur Benton, PhD, developed tests for brain-impaired and dementia patients and internationally recognized for research on aphasia; Richard Fincham, neurologist; Adolph Sahs, Chairman of the Department of Neurology, one of the four founding members of the American Academy of Neurology (AAN); Maurice van Allen, a close friend of Bob's; Bob Joynt.

MERRY CHRISTMAS   from the JOYNTS
                                                    1965

Joynt family, 1965. *Left to right:* Bob, Margaret, Kathy, Bobby, Tricia, Mary, Anne, Tom.

Joynt family, 1978. *Left to right:* Kathy, Anne, Bobby, Tricia, Bob, Mary, Tom, Margaret.

Adolph Sahs, Chairman of Neurology, University of Iowa College of Medicine.

Rex Ingram, Chairman of Anatomy, University of Iowa College of Medicine.

Arthur Benton, Professor of Psychology, University of Iowa.

Department of Neurology, University of Iowa College of Medicine, 1962. *Left to right, first row:* Arthur L. Benton, Edward W. Sybil, Adolph H. Sahs, Maurice W. Van Allen, Robert J. Joynt; *second row:* Alan O. Hage, Robert J. Gumnit, William W. Kaelber, James A. Shepherd, Riyad R. Kalifeh, Otfried Spreen; *third row:* Richard A. Calkins, Richard W. Fincham, Harry W. Rein, Thomas E. Gretter, Vincent Taormina, Charles A. Cape.

Original members of Department of Neurology, University of Rochester, 1966. *Left to right, first row:* Paul Garvey, Bob Joynt, Richard Satran; *second row:* David Marsh, David Goldblatt, Marvin Goldstein, Donald Castle.

Ten-year anniversary of Department of Neurology, University of Rochester, 1975.

Bob and Margaret, 1976.

Past presidents of the American Academy of Neurology (AAN). Bob Joynt (*first row, left*). Bob served as president of the AAN from 1977 to 1979.

Past presidents of the American Neurological Association, 1988. Bob Joynt, *first row, second from left.*

Inauguration as dean of the University of Rochester School of
Medicine and Dentistry, pictured with keynote speaker Sir Roger
Bannister, 1985.

At his desk, 1987.

Bob in famous brain hat with McCollister "Mac" Evarts before
Dr. Evarts left to become Dean of the College of Medicine, The
Pennsylvania State University and The Milton S. Hershey Medical
Center in Hershey, Pennsylvania.

Leaders at UR Medical Center, 1990. *Left to right:* Marshall Lichtman, Dean of Medical School; Bob Joynt, Vice President for Health Affairs; Sheila Ryan, Dean of Nursing; Paul Griner, General Director and CEO of Strong Memorial Hospital.

Three deans of the University of Rochester School of Medicine and Dentistry. *Left to right:* Robert Joynt, Lowell Goldsmith, Marshall A. Lichtman.

Bob and Margaret, 1991.

Close friends. *Left to right, first row:* Genevieve Solazzo, Ethan Welch, Bobbie Wilson; *second row,* Janet Welch, Bob, Margaret, Michael Solazzo.

Bob and Father Dan Tormey on La Trappe Creek Society sailing trip.

Bob and Margaret, American Heart Association's Heart Ball, 1995.

Symposium on Presidential Disability and the 25th Amendment. President Gerald Ford (first row, seventh from left); James Toole (first row, eighth from left), coauthor of Presidential Disability; Senator Birch Bayh (first row, left), Bob Joynt (second row, ninth from left). November 1995.

Bob and Margaret with Bob's three sisters and spouses, 1997.

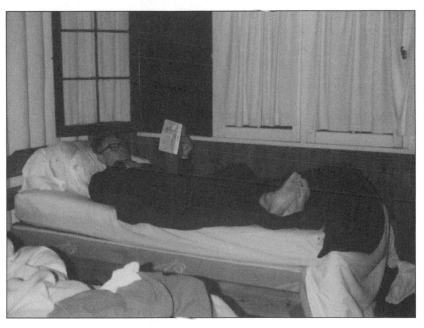

Bob on vacation at Leech Lake, Minnesota.

Joynt grandchildren, 1988. *Left to right, first row:* Lilly Pieper, Madeleine Pieper; *second row,* Phoebe Joynt, Margaret, Cate Goodman, Bob, Isabella Joynt; *third row,* Robert Joynt, Robert Wodarski, Michael Wodarski, Patrick Joynt.

Joynt Christmas, 2005, children and grandchildren. *Left to right, first row:* Lilly Pieper, Phoebe Joynt, Cate Goodman, Isabella Joynt, Madeleine Pieper; *second row,* Michael Wodarski, Ed Wodarski, Bob, Margaret, Rob Wodarski; *third row,* Kathy, Anne, Tricia, Mary, Ye-Yeng; *fourth row,* Michael Pieper, Betsy Joynt, Tom, Don Goodman, Robert Joynt, Bobby, Patrick Joynt.

Bob with sons and sons-in-law sailing with La Trappe Creek Society.
Left to right: Ed Wodarski, Michael Pieper, Bob Joynt, Tom Joynt,
Bobby Joynt.

Kayaking on Keuka Lake.

The "gourmet group," 2000. *Left to right:* Bob Joynt, Margaret Joynt, John Kuiper, Ellen Kuiper, Don Reiff, Mary Reiff, Polly Huntsberger, Don Huntsberger, Connie Klein, Bob Klein, in Adare, Ireland, the birthplace of Margaret's grandmother and great-grandmother.

Bob in London. "I think, I think . . . maybe I'll write a neurological
Sherlockian pastiche. . . ."

12

"LOW INTELLECT IN HIGH PLACES"

It's a saucy title for an after-dinner speech, and it always attracted a big crowd. Who wouldn't want to hear the distinguished neurologist Dr. Robert J. Joynt, *raconteur non pareil*, talk about politics—in a manner that promised to puncture the pompous.

Indeed, what Dr. Bob gave his eager listeners were lessons in history—stories of world leaders weakened by human frailty or accidents of fate. Whether he was talking about Britain's mad King George III or a troubled Ronald Reagan, Dr. Bob's listeners were left with a sobering message: the captains of the world's ships of state are, like all of us, exquisitely vulnerable. In later talks, he would raise this question: In troubled times, does our Constitution adequately protect us from political chaos when disaster strikes our president?

Dr. Bob knew—as well as any history professor—what he was talking about. He had grown up in a politically active family and his fascination with politics, past and present, was lifelong. He also had immersed himself in the history of medicine, initiating a course in its study at UR's medical school. The two interests frequently intertwined; as an invited lecturer at Columbia University's medical school, for example, he chose to focus on how history may have been affected by the health issues experienced by heads of state during World War I and World War II.

≈ ≈ ≈

"Who's Minding the World?" was the question Dr. Bob raised in a 1996 editorial in *JAMA*. History is changed by accidents, he pointed out, and by human frailty, as when presidents face heart attacks, strokes, severe stress, and assassins' bullets, all of which had affected American presidents in recent decades. If the president *and* the vice president were seriously disabled, could the center hold?

The question had been asked thirty years earlier. Concern about presidential succession protocol had heated in 1963 after the assassination of President Kennedy in Dallas as Vice President Johnson was flying back from Texas. That concern approached the boiling point when General Alexander Haig issued this curt statement to the press as the shocking news broke: "I am in control here at the White House." A year later, President Lyndon Johnson reminded Congress: "A nation bearing the responsibilities we are privileged to bear . . . cannot justify the appalling gamble of entrusting its security to the immobilized hands or uncomprehending mind of a Commander-in-Chief unable to command."

Two years later, Congress would begin wrestling with the question, Could a Constitutional amendment clarify the clouded issue? The decision: Perhaps. Let's look at the question more closely.

☙ ☙ ☙

Those who heard Dr. Bob's talks in the '90s on the subject of presidential succession may have forgotten details of the Twenty-Fifth Amendment to the Constitution. Ratified by Congress in 1967, it was designed to clarify succession procedures, focusing in particular on procedures to determine what constitutes "presidential disability." New York State Representative Kenneth Keating had introduced the amendment to Congress in partnership with Senator Estes Kefauver of Tennessee. After months of intense debate, the final draft, written by Senator Birch Bayh and Herbert Brownell, Eisenhower's attorney general, was ratified.

Among other measures, the Twenty-Fifth Amendment calls for medical evaluation to determine presidential incapacity, but is vague about specifics. That vagueness, many came to believe, is the amendment's Achilles' heel. What kind of medical evaluation is appropriate? Who will be the evaluator? The president's own doctor? A panel of medical experts? A psychiatrist or a neurologist? What about the long-honored principal of physician-patient confidentiality? The pros and cons of the issue were (and still are) debated, sometimes with rancor.

In his '96 *JAMA* editorial "Who's Minding the World?" Dr. Joynt suggests that one of the Twenty-Fifth Amendment's failures is charging the vice president to start determination of disability proceedings against the president that he or she is serving, an action that may suggest a possible coup d'état. Whatever the reason, the author points out that in similar situations the vice president has been reluctant to accept the responsibility of starting proceedings against the disabled president.

?? ?? ??

As the twentieth century drew to a close, concern over who had the right to declare a president incompetent once again became an issue. Questions raised a decade earlier over President Reagan's mental health were still fresh. With the 2000 presidential elections looming, one commentator referenced a popular TV game show of the time to convey the urgency of the issue: "The $64,000 question is: Who's going to determine whether or not a President is disabled?"

As Dr. Joynt would point out pragmatically in his *JAMA* editorial: "the position and authority of the [president's] staff are dependent on the continuing and active presence of the president. They would be loath to point out personal frailties to the incumbent and to make these frailties known to the public"—as had happened in the cases of Woodrow Wilson and FDR.

In 1994, President Jimmy Carter proposed that a "working panel" be convened to examine the Twenty-Fifth Amendment's effectiveness. For help in selecting the panel members he turned to the American Academy of Neurology. In January 1995, forty-seven men and three women, including President Carter, physicians (including the doctors for the three living presidents), scientists, lawyers, philanthropists, historians, and journalists, gathered at the Carter Center in Atlanta for a three-day examination of the perceived problem. Dr. Robert Joynt was among the fifty chosen.

Nine months later the group, modified by the presence of President Gerald Ford, met again for three days at Wake Forest University to continue the discussion. Finally, early in December 1996, the working group met at the White House Conference Center to offer its report. The majority opinion: "revision or augmentation of the amendment appears to be impractical and might create greater problems than it sought to correct."

The end result of the working group's deliberations was the 2001 publication by the University of Rochester Press of a massive book, nearly six hundred pages, entitled *Presidential Disability:*

Papers, Discussions, and Recommendations on the Twenty-Fifth Amendment and Issues of Inability and Disability in Presidents of the United States. The coeditors were James E. Toole and Robert J. Joynt.

Both editors were experts on the subject of presidential disabilities and each added luster to the deliberations. Dr. Bob we know well. Dr. Toole was then professor of neurology and director of the Stroke Research Center at Wake Forest University, as well as past president of the World Federation of Neurology. Both men had led major organizations in their specialty.

Margaret Joynt remembers the stacks of paper, official transcriptions generated by the two conferences, that arrived later that year at Dr. Bob's office—at a time when her husband's eyesight, never as good as 50/50, was much weakened and his eyeglasses thick. Now he faced a mountain of papers: introductory letters from Presidents Clinton and Ford, every speech from the nine cumulative days of the two conferences, as well as the question-and-answer sessions that followed. Here was the book's foreword, preface, and scholarly introduction. Lists of committee members proliferated, as well as the names of guests and observers. Most important of all, here were the committees' recommendations—plus the resulting spirited commentary. The bibliography would eventually fill seven pages, the vast index twelve pages.

Of course, the editors were not responsible for checking every fact and every citation; much of that happened elsewhere. But editor Bob read every word of the galley proof, his wife insists. He also was the interface, the binding agent, between the Carter Center and Wake Forest conference leaders and the University of Rochester Press. He had to know everything the massive book contained—and he did.

Dr. Bob's six-year involvement with the threefold conference and the publication of its findings reinforced all that he knew already about how leaders' vulnerabilities could affect history. Taking the stories to the podium, he made history live for eager audiences as he told the stories of Woodrow Wilson, whose wife was the country's de facto president for several weeks in the 1920s; of FDR and his struggles with polio and its aftereffects; of Churchill's father, a political power eventually demented by syphilis; of John Kennedy and his struggle with Addison's disease and amphetamines. Audiences always seemed to fall under the spell of this genial Irish storyteller. This time the tales he told were all true.

As for the Twenty-Fifth Amendment, Mrs. Joynt says her husband would have agreed with *New York Times* journalist Tom Wicker, who represented the working group's majority opinion with this story: "The congregation of a country church was fiercely divided over whether or not to add another window to the chancel for the sake of symmetry. Bad feelings were rampant. Finally a church meeting was called to settle the question. Great and acrimonious debate followed. At last, an old fellow rose in the back row and said, gruffly, 'Preacher, I move we leave them windows alone.'"[1]

After three long sessions, the committee reached an agreement that matched the suggestion of the old fellow in Wicker's story. At least for now, the Twenty-Fifth Amendment to the Constitution on issues of presidential succession stands as ratified.

13

STALKING SHERLOCK HOLMES

"My mind . . . rebels at stagnation. Give me problems, give me
work, give me the most abstruse cryptogram or the most intricate
analysis, and I am in my own proper atmosphere."

—Sherlock Holmes, *The Sign of Four*

Young Bob Joynt met Sherlock Holmes in the reading room of the Le Mars Public Library. With the turning of each page of *The Adventure of the Speckled Band,* the boy's enthrallment deepened. Sunny Iowa afternoons faded away as he slipped quietly into the dark world of Victorian London and began slinking along the city's lowest, vilest alleys. His invisible companion, the tall man with the pungent pipe and the long cloak, challenged the boy to keep pace, not with longer strides, but mentally.

Always there were questions for the boy to consider. Who might have dropped the pale-blue unsigned note at the door of 221B Baker Street? That exotic, spicy odor that suddenly assailed the nose—could the boy detect its presence? What monster lurking in the midnight darkness had left its fresh prints on the moor near the Baskervilles' estate? Think, boy, think! Above all, pay attention! Data, data, data: that's what's important.

If the love affair began early, it lasted right up to the end. In his last years, Dr. Bob assumed the voice of Arthur Conan Doyle in a series of six mysteries published in the journal *Neurology.* The key to solving each of these criminal puzzles required Sherlock (and the reader) to recognize a significant clue based on a specific neurological symptom. Much more on that later.

ᴥ ᴥ ᴥ

We've seen that young Bob Joynt's household had a strong medical focus: the dentist father, uncles who were doctors, aunts who were nurses. Why wouldn't the boy be deeply drawn into these tales told by the world-famous storyteller? For a few hours a week, Bob was swept away from rural Iowa, transported by Arthur Conan Doyle, an Irishman (an *Irishman!*). Even better, an Irishman who was a doctor!

Sir Arthur held degrees from schools of medicine in Edinburgh and Vienna. An adventurer who loved the sea (as did our Dr. Bob), Doyle in his early years served as a doctor on a Greenland whaler and later as a ship's surgeon on a voyage to South Africa. On his return from the latter trip, he completed an advanced degree in Scotland on the subject of *tabes dorsalis* (or *syphilitic myelopathy*), the inability to coordinate bodily movements due to syphilis of the spinal cord. In 1890, Dr. Doyle left private practice to study ophthalmology in Vienna, eventually setting up practice in that specialty at No. 2 Wimpole Street in London.[1]

The link between the famous author's literary output and medicine is strong. As early as his medical student days in Scotland and shortly after his African trip, Doyle began writing mysteries—the first, a short story set in Africa, "The Mystery of Sasassa Valley." His first medical paper was published in 1879 in the *British Medical Journal*; its subject: "Geisemonium as a Poison." More than one hundred years later, the *London Daily Telegraph* suggested the study might be useful in the case of an alleged murder then being investigated.

Sir Arthur's grand ascension in England's literary and social world must be seen against its dark Victorian background, for the boy had been raised in a slum tenement, a come-down for a family of Irish patriots who in better times had entertained well-known writers and artists, including Thackeray, Rosetti, and Millais. Unfortunately, Arthur's father, Charles, was both an epileptic and alcoholic. The two demons were responsible for his institutionalization and death in an asylum for the insane and the family's collapse. The saving hand for the young boy was extended by an uncle, who provided him with a solid Jesuit education—preparation for a life in a faith that Conan Doyle would soon reject.

This dramatic family saga must have fascinated the boy who was reading so avidly in the Le Mars library during those long summer afternoons. There was so much Irishness in the story—and so much of the world of medicine that suffused the boy's own warm and supportive home life. In dark contrast, in Conan Doyle's world, father and son were locked in conflict—the incurable, poverty-stricken Charles, and Arthur, the world-famous literary lion and physician.

All of Dr. Bob's family—and most of his friends and colleagues—would come to know about his love of all things relating to Sherlock, Watson, and Conan Doyle. On leaving Cambridge after his Fulbright year, his friends had presented him with a Meerschaum pipe, a treasured totem of the great detective that remained on his office desk ever after.

Mary Joynt Wodarski, anointed as her father's special Holmesian pal among the Joynt offspring, recalls accompanying him to a convention of devotees in Cleveland. "It was a sight!" she says, with some of the faithful arriving in appropriate period garb: Sherlock lookalikes, Eastern exotics, a few sultry and mysterious women, scruffy (if rather outsize) urchins, and—of course—doctors. As a teenager, about to leave for college, Mary was impressed at the seriousness of the presentations and their variety. An avid cook herself now, she especially remembers the lecture on food and drink of the period, based on the presenter's study of all the Sherlock stories—and late evenings spent watching the early black-and-white Holmes films with her father and bowls of popcorn.

❧   ❧   ❧

All this devotion found its logical outlet in 2006 when the first of Dr. Joynt's Sherlock Holmes tales appeared in the journal *Neurology* in the section "Reflections: Neurology and the Humanities." Written in the distinctive voice of Dr. John Watson, Sherlock's amanuensis and partner in crime solving, the tales draw on Dr. Bob's deep knowledge of neurology and human nature, and his familiarity with the literary style he was mirroring. The titles include "The Case of the Colored Crystals," "The Case of the Misguided Squire," "The Case of the Reed in the Breeze," "The Case of the Collapsing Man," "The Silent Witness and Charcot's Hat," and "The Case of the Locked House: The Unfinished Mystery," the last story published posthumously.

Listen for a moment, if you will, as Bob Joynt channels Arthur Conan Doyle in his 2006 tale "The Case of the Reed in the Breeze." Perhaps you'll catch the style and the pleasure Dr. Bob took in re-creating Dr. Watson's famous voice. As the story begins, the good doctor is once again back at 221B Baker Street, with its *"welter of test tubes and notebooks, and with the noisome aroma of Holmes' latest tobacco."*

Enter Mrs. Hudson, Holmes's housekeeper, leading a lady in distress. *"The young woman was very anxious, indeed. She was well, but not expensively, dressed. She sat down in a proffered chair and immediately bent her head forward and sobbed, 'We are ruined, we are ruined.'*

"Watson, some brandy for our young friend," the famous sleuth orders. Then he turns to the sobbing woman: *"Please take some brandy, gather your thoughts, and tell us about the troubling matter."* The trouble, Holmes learns, involves an important briefcase stolen during a brutal attack on the woman's husband; its contents, in the wrong hands, could bring disaster to a major company.

A witness to the attack is soon identified and questioned by Holmes in London's rough-and-tough Billingsgate fish market. *"Well, guv'nor . . . I saw the man running with the case, and I saw our young friend lying on the pavement. I put two and two together and figured the man had snatched the case and took off. Guv'nor, I am no runner as you can see by the size of my middle. The thief was no speeder either. But he went into that dark alley there . . . he was stumbling and swaying like my old lady on Saturday night. Once he stopped, and he swayed like a reed in the breeze. Then I lost him."*

Not for the first time, the great detective turns for help to his brother Mycroft, a mysterious and reclusive figure linked to Scotland Yard; they dine together that evening at Mycroft's sanctum, the Diogenes Club. The next morning, Holmes meets with Dr. Watson; he carries a book and is in a highly excited state. Watson inquires about the meeting with Mycroft and the following exchange ensues:

It was, says Holmes, *"Capital, Watson, capital. . . . Mycroft had arranged a dinner with two other members, a Dr. Hughlings Jackson and Sir William Gowers, both eccentric in their own way, but very personable. Perhaps you have heard of them?"*

"I gasped. They are two of the foremost neurologists in our profession. Jackson is the leading figure at Queen Square. Gowers has written the standard text . . . and was knighted by our dear Queen in her Diamond Jubilee year. Holmes, you were in heady company."

It was indeed a most fortuitous evening, Holmes tells Watson. After he had shared details of the case of the missing portfolio with the eminent doctors, they directed him to the club's library and a particular volume, *Diseases of the Nervous System*. There they marked a section under the heading "Locomotor Ataxy," information that

Holmes shares with Watson: *"The characteristic in-coordination of movement . . . may render difficult the maintenance of equilibrium when the base of support is narrowed by the feet being placed closely together . . . if then the eyes are closed the patient sways, and tends to fall. . . . The early defect of in-coordination may be discovered by the patient when he walks in the dark."*

Armed with this information, Holmes has the police round up fifty carters from the fish market, a motley and smelly crew, who are lined up in rows. Dr. Watson, as the medical man in charge, has each suspect in turn stand at attention and close his eyes. The third man in the second row closes his eyes, lurches back and forth, and nearly falls. Watson turns triumphantly: *"This is your man, Holmes."* A quick search through the man's cart reveals the missing leather case, now smelling highly of fish.

The story concludes: *"In the hansom cab on their way back to Baker Street, Holmes turned to me and said, 'Watson, for your invaluable help in expediting that search, I have purchased two tickets tonight for a performance of some of Scarlatti's works, where we can unburden ourselves from some of the sights, sounds, and smells of the day.'"*

ᴥ   ᴥ   ᴥ

The last of Dr. Bob's Sherlock Holmes stories lay unfinished in his computer until it was discovered in 2012, after his death, by his longtime assistant Nancy Baldwin. Unfinished, yes, but not for long. In an inspirational move by *Neurology* editor Robert Gross and managing editor Kathy Joynt Pieper, the incomplete story was published in the journal and readers were invited to compose an ending—in Conan Doyle's characteristic style and with a neurological conclusion. An editorial panel selected and published the top four entries; readers picked the winner. "The Case of the Locked House: The Finished Mystery" appeared in *Neurology* with three coauthors, Dr. Joynt and the two neurologists (one from London, the other from Australia) who collaborated on the winning entry.

Gerald Honch, UR Professor Emeritus of Neurology, caught the Holmes fever directly from the man who hired him fifty years ago. In gratitude, at the end of his residency Honch presented his mentor with Baring-Gould's two-volume annotated collection of Conan Doyle's works. He also introduced UR's renowned neurologist to the members of Rochester Row, the city's Sherlockian Society (whose name comes from a passage in *The Sign of Four*). The members had the pleasure of hearing Dr. Bob read aloud one of his own Sherlock Holmes mysteries.

෨ ෨ ෨

Sherlock Holmes's advice is still relevant a century after it was written, especially for medical students. Dr. Bob could have quoted Holmes verbatim during the classes for neurology residents, for which he was so well known and which were so eagerly attended:

> "Data! Data! Data! . . . I can't make bricks without clay."
> —*The Adventure of the Copper Beeches*
> "It is a capital mistake to theorize before one has data. Insensibly one begins to twist facts to suit theories."
> —*A Scandal in Bohemia*
> "You see, but you do not observe. The distinction is clear."
> —*A Scandal in Bohemia*
> "There is nothing more deceptive than an obvious fact."
> —*The Sign of Four*
> "When you have eliminated the impossible, whatever remains, *however impossible*, must be the truth."
> —*The Sign of Four*

෨ ෨ ෨

Dr. Bob treasured the world of the imagination, so richly revealed in Conan Doyle's mysteries and in those by other master crime writers. But his feet were firmly planted in reality, the world he lived in every day, where money, medicine, and politics rubbed shoulders, sometimes painfully. At the end of one of the convivial dinners with colleagues that Dr. Bob so very much enjoyed, could he have resisted sharing this wry Holmes *bon mot* from *A Study in Scarlet*? Here's how the world's greatest detective describes his unusual profession: *"I listen to their story, they listen to my comments, and then I pocket my fee."*

14

DEAN JOYNT TAKES THE HELM

"I grew up in a household where politics was a major part of our lives. My father wanted me to go into politics and my mother wanted me to go into medicine. When I became Dean of a medical school, I believed I had satisfied both of their aspirations."
—Robert J. Joynt, "Comments," *Neurology* (2003)

In 1984, Dr. Bob was busy leading the Department of Neurology to new heights when he received a rather unexpected summons from UR President Robert Sproull. A major shift in Medical Center leadership was about to occur. The dean and vice president for health affairs, Frank Young, was leaving—also rather unexpectedly—for Washington, where he would become the new commissioner of the Food and Drug Administration. Would Bob come to the rescue and become acting dean?

It must have been a tough question to answer. All the evidence points to the fact that Dr. Bob loved being chairman of the department he'd founded. Why did he agree to this (perhaps temporary) move up the career ladder? Perhaps he'd come to realize that he'd achieved the goal he'd set for himself when he, Margaret, and the family arrived in Rochester: to build the best Department of Neurology in the country. Perhaps he was ready for another challenge. Certainly he was secure in the knowledge that with Berch Griggs as the new chairman, the department would be in good hands. Whatever the reasons, Dr. Bob's answer to President Sproull was yes.

≥≥   ≥≥   ≥≥

A few months later, the University of Rochester had a new president: Dennis O'Brien, recruited from Bucknell University. On his arrival, O'Brien immediately faced major problems on almost all fronts. His mission from UR trustees was to strengthen the undergraduate program and improve matriculation rates. A recent decision among Ivy League colleges to move toward greater student diversity was funneling students away from Rochester (where the undergraduate admission policy had always been open) and admissions were down. That situation needed fixing.

At the same time, a dark cloud had settled over the university's financial situation. An endowment that was once among the highest in the nation had been rocked by an investment policy that was proving to be unwise, if not disastrous. Major holdings in blue-chip stocks ("the nifty fifty") had been sold, with 20 percent reinvested in new, smaller companies that seemed to promise great future growth. That promise was not being fulfilled. Shifting back to a more conservative portfolio would be difficult; suddenly selling even 10 percent of the endowment's holdings in the new companies would only deflate their market value. How to save and reinvigorate the portfolio was an open question.

More problems were roiling the waters over at Crittenden Boulevard, where Strong Memorial Hospital and the schools of medicine, dentistry, and nursing were facing major environmental change. Big money, in the form of government programs (Medicare, Medicaid), third-party payers, and increased federal research funding, was forcing changes within what had been a solid, conservative community of medical academics, practitioners, and scientists. The shrinking endowment raised budgetary concerns, since typically 40 percent of UR endowment income goes to the Medical Center.

Change was everywhere during those years. The revolution in science that had begun after World War II was in full flood. Suddenly this relatively quiet academic community was confronting an explosion in medical advances, the arrival of complex new technologies, and ever-increasing rules and regulations. Adding to the stress, doctors and staff at Strong Memorial Hospital were facing a medical monster, terrifying and mysterious, that was wreaking havoc in the community—HIV/AIDS.

Understandably, tensions within the Medical Center often were high. With no dean or director in place, who would lead them?

❧　　❧　　❧

For UR's medical community and for the new President O'Brien, this was the overriding question. Who would succeed Frank Young—and what would be the nature of that position now? Young had been a powerhouse. As both dean and director of the UR Medical Center, he had achieved much, including elevating both leadership posts—but some faculty were still smarting over what they saw as his overreaching style.

Dennis O'Brien, recalling those years, said that his conversations with leaders at other universities and with the Medical Center faculty convinced him that it would be a mistake to appoint a dean who would replicate Frank Young's "one-man-band" style. Instead, he chose to de-escalate the model, focusing on the deanship and changing the title of vice president to vice provost for health affairs. The man he chose for the post was acting dean Robert Joynt. It was, he would say later, "the best appointment I ever made."

O'Brien believes leaders come in two forms: earth shakers and earth smoothers. "Frank Young had been an earth shaker. Now what we needed was an earth smoother—and nobody could be a better earth smoother than Bob Joynt. Bob was not only respected and honored at the Medical Center—he was actually beloved. . . . I recall talking with a man who said to me, 'If I could nominate one person in the country to serve on the Supreme Court, it would be Bob Joynt.'"

A year later, and sixty years after the founding the School of Medicine and Dentistry, Dr. Robert Joynt became the venerable school's fifth dean. He couldn't have been more pleased with the inaugural ceremony. His friend, Donald Hunsberger, Eastman School of Music professor, brought students of his wind ensemble to provide the music. As planning for the ceremony began, President O'Brien had made clear that he wanted an event full of optimism, a portent of great things to come for both the school and the university—a "feel-good" celebration in the midst of troublesome times. "Find a really good speaker," he urged Dr. Bob. "Would Sir Roger Bannister do?" asked the dean to be.

In 1985, a celebrity glow still surrounded Sir Roger, who had become a sports world hero thirty-one year years earlier as the first to break the four-minute-mile record. Now the famous runner was a distinguished neurologist at London's Queen Square Hospital and master of Pembroke College at Oxford. Dr. and Mrs. Joynt had been entertained by Sir Roger and his wife Dame Moira during their recent sabbatical in London (as they had been, sequentially, by the leaders of London's major hospitals where Bob had been guest lecturer). The invitation to the Bannisters to come to Rochester for the new dean's installation quickly was accepted. Amidst a flurry of activity, Dr. Bob's assistant, Nancy Baldwin, and her crew turned the reception hall at nearby St. Agnes School into a British garden, with trees, flowers, cucumber sandwiches, strawberries and cream, champagne, and an Irish band. It was, according to all reports, a celebration to remember.

?◆   ?◆   ?◆

As the School of Medicine and Dentistry's fifth dean, Bob had three exceptional men to help him guide the ship through these challenging times. Calling on the leadership model that had helped make the Department of Neurology nationally known, he followed his own rule: "Pick talented people and then get out of their way." As associate dean for education he had the cardiologist Jules Cohen, a man respected by both students and faculty—and a colleague who matched Bob's sense of humor with his own variety of wit. To lead the school's already impressive research program, Dean Bob had Marshall Lichtman, associate dean for academic affairs and research. Lichtman is a nationally known hematologist who then was strengthening research efforts and developing the Medical Center's bone-marrow transplantation program. Providing liaison with Strong Memorial Hospital was the associate dean for clinical affairs, the well-respected urologist Irwin Frank.

For Dean Bob and his team, the problem of finding money to support the faculty was ever present. At the time of Bob's appointment, annual figures relating to clinical care and research had expanded exponentially, whereas the medical school budget, restrained by a relatively fixed number of students, showed only modest growth. A 1984 letter to President O'Brien states the problem succinctly. Dean Bob writes: "Heads of Medical Center academic departments are not only expected to dance, but provide their own music." In other words, each one had to teach, conduct research, care for patients, get grants, and generate patient-related income.

As early as his arrival in Rochester, Dr. Bob had understood the challenges facing the School of Medicine and Dentistry. In 1975, he addressed "the urge to grow and the urge to stay small" in an essay published at the time of the medical school's twenty-fifth anniversary in *To Each His Farthest Star*. Using data, charts, and amusing cartoons, he made the point that growth was winning; faculty numbers, for example, had increased from 95 in 1946 to 878 in 1974. Ten years later, during Bob's deanship, Rochester would rank seventeenth in the nation in NIH funding.

For Dean Bob, ensuring that the school would remain strong in the presence of often conflicting interests was key. His 1984 letter to President O'Brien states the case: "In any reading about academic medical centers, the medical school is the key element. This is particularly true at Rochester, where most of our reputation and tradition is in education and research. . . . The sticky problem remains as to how costs, revenues, and programs involving all elements of the Medical Center are to be decided."

❧   ❧   ❧

During the early '80s, newness and change seemed to be everywhere. The Medical Center welcomed the arrival of MRI and PET scanning technology, the sophisticated new methods of imaging the body, its bones, brain, and organs. A university plan to develop the NYS Center for Advanced Optical Technology promised to include a medical component. For Jules Cohen and his cadre of teaching professors, all these rapidly announced advances in medical science came with an educational consequence. As they prepared for each new class of medical students, they would have to update their lectures, often radically, to include this new information.

As the AIDS epidemic advanced across the region, spreading fear and confusion, the Medical Center's executive committee decided to commit a major portion of the second floor of U-Wing to an AIDS Center, with a projected cost of $1 million, funded by a federal grant secured by Lichtman. The effort would involve the whole medical enterprise: hospital, school, and various research teams.

At the same time, resurrecting the feminist message of Rochester's Susan B. Anthony, women faculty across all the colleges of the university—then approaching one hundred in number—were organizing for equal pay and equal respect. Dean Bob, who lived with four daughters and an outspoken wife with a law degree, understood what the women were talking about. He stepped up to the plate and appointed the first woman to chair a department at the medical school: scientist Barbara Iglewski in microbiology.

All these changes were made more difficult by what may have been the most sweeping change of all: computerization across the whole university. Difficult as it is to imagine now, teaching a new technology to thousands of men and women used to typewriters and file cabinets was not easy. It was particularly difficult within this community where most people were already very busy, working long hours—many of them dealing with life-and-death issues.

During the next four years, as challenges came and were met, Dean Bob stayed steady at the helm, steering a straight course. Paul Griner, then CEO of Strong Memorial Hospital, says in retrospect: "With Bob at the helm, the school maintained a sense of values very similar to those in play when George Whipple was dean, a time when the relationship between student and teacher was valued. I think that was the most important element in Bob's tenure."

❧   ❧   ❧

The Joynt family was very much part of these deanship years, as they would be throughout Dr. Bob's career. As Ralph Jozefowicz, himself a much-loved professor, remembers: "Bob would have parties at his house all the time, and the family was always involved. He always hosted the Christmas party and scheduled the Journal Club monthly meeting around St. Patrick's Day so there could be a party. I believe Bob was happiest when he saw that other people were happy."

Barney Stern at the University of Maryland recalls a postresidency reunion with his family at the Joynts' home. "I'll never forget seeing Bob, this world-renowned figure, kneeling down to be at eye level with my daughters and saying, 'Just call me Bob.' Bob always said, 'family first,' a phrase I use to this day with my students and residents, and even my colleagues."

Wouldn't you think all this adulation would go straight to the head? Not when the head in question was Bob Joynt's. His colleague Ira Shoulson was in the dean's office late one afternoon when Bob took an after-hours phone call. A woman from the suburbs was looking for a speaker for her women's group. "I don't want anyone lower than a dean," she said, rather imperiously. Dr. Shoulson tried to stifle his laughter when he heard Bob's reply: "Madam, there is no one lower than a dean."

❧   ❧   ❧

The former Strong Memorial Hospital CEO Paul Griner believes that Dr. Bob's years as dean were his happiest years: "In my mind, Bob was the quintessential dean. He loved it, he reveled in it." Key to that joy was the greater opportunity he had to interact with the students. Once-a-week pizza parties with a dozen students were occasions for teaching, fellowship, and laughter; now, years later, many graduates remember them as a highlight of their student days.

Dr. Bob's longtime editorial assistant Nancy Baldwin wondered at the time whether the new job would change him. "Don't worry," he told her. "I'm going to continue to wear my button-down shirt and khakis." He may have become a nationally known figure, but he would never lose his "regular guy" disguise.

No doubt it was the medical students and residents, his family, his close friends and colleagues, and his sense of humor that saw Dean Joynt through what must have been many trying days. Always, he could see the amusing side. A quick look through his letters of that period often proves the point.

Here's an example: At a time when Strong Memorial had just installed a new machine to improve leucocyte differential counts in the hematology lab, Associate Dean Marshall Lichtman sent the following wistful note to Dean Joynt: "You neurologists are lucky. I've just been replaced by a computer algorithm." Dean Bob's response: "We now have all sorts of devices to quantitate the neurological examination. Technology has put *rigor* into Neurology, but also, unfortunately, *mortis*."

OK, it'll never make *Comedy Central*. But as an example of scientists' spur-of-the-moment humor, it's not bad.

VICE PRESIDENT JOYNT'S TEAM
BUILDS FOR THE FUTURE

"A transition period is a period between two transition periods."
—George Stigler, Nobel Memorial
Prize in Economics, 1982

A bold new chapter in the history of the University of Rochester opened on January 1, 1990, when Dr. Robert J. Joynt became Vice President for Health Affairs at the University of Rochester. As VP, Dr. Bob now stood alone at the top of an integrated set of health facilities and programs[1]—the School of Medicine and Dentistry, the School of Nursing, and Strong Memorial Hospital—known collectively as the University of Rochester Medical Center. Often referred to by its acronym, URMC, the Medical Center serves as a national model for outstanding healthcare, research, and medical education.

This leadership configuration—a pyramid topped by a vice president for health affairs—was forged just as the storm of circumstances already buffeting health care costs, medical education, and the ability to provide good patient care was gathering strength. Effective communication between the River Campus and the Medical Center during these fraught times was more essential than ever. This new model directly linked the vice president for health affairs, representing both the schools and the hospital, with the president of the university, ensuring that the medical center had a continuing voice at the trustees' table.

That voice would have to come from a seasoned diplomat, someone who could negotiate effectively among powerful interests. If the voice also could be soothing and supportive rather than insistent, temperate with a talent for team-building, caring rather than confrontational, and wise with eyes on the future, so much the better. Only one person seemed to meet those extraordinary expectations: our Dr. Bob, then dean and vice provost. All his skills soon would be put to the test.

Around the country, conflicts were breaking out between medical schools and teaching hospitals when each had separate governing bodies. Paul Griner, then CEO of Strong Memorial Hospital, recalls: "It was important that we be able to speak with one voice both internally, within the university, and externally, when dealing with state and federal authorities, national organizations in the health field, and suppliers. We were fortunate that our medical school, nursing school, and hospital were under the same governance structure, the university's board of trustees. That made for coordinated planning and philosophy."

Internally, there were clear advantages to elevating a single figure to the top of the leadership pyramid. As Peter Robinson, then director for strategic planning for the hospital, points out: "At the time there was enormous frustration with a system that was broken in terms of how the medical school and hospital interacted. Typifying that dysfunction was the way negotiations were handled for recruiting and funding clinical leaders, particularly the chairs of departments whose costs were born proportionately by school and hospital."

Every advantage would need to be optimized as Dr. Bob and his team faced the challenges presented by this new decade.

~   ~   ~

As VP, Dr. Bob was charged with leading the institution through an ever-more turbulent environment. Academic medical centers and their teaching hospitals stood at a crossroads, as Griner has pointed out. Change was coming, dramatic and exaggerated. An uncoordinated national healthcare system was resulting in double-digit increases in health insurance costs. Promising research projects stalled as formerly robust federal funding for biomedical research was threatened, a problem exacerbated by a decrease in university endowment spending.

Rochester, whose style of community-rated healthcare and careful management of the number of hospital beds[2] had been acclaimed as a model for the nation, now saw the slow disintegration of what had been a strong partnership among industry, healthcare providers, and insurers. Competition for the healthcare dollar, not cooperation, was about to take over.

Rochester was far from alone in facing disruptions from the forces of change. At that time, the editor of *Rochester Medicine*,[3] the school's alumni magazine, had asked several URMC alumni, then leading other medical centers, to comment on the challenges facing their institutions. All were alike in their comments: things were tough and getting tougher.

William A. Peck, MD, then dean of the medical school at Washington University and currently director of its Center for Health Policy, said it clearly: "A price-competitive marketplace is making it more and more difficult for academic health centers to subsidize education, research, and the care of large numbers of the uninsured whom we are called upon to treat." From the University of California, San Francisco, Dean of the School of Medicine Joseph B. Martin[4] reported: "I spend half my time dealing with issues of re-engineering within our institution." And at Hershey Medical Center, Vice President for Health Affairs C. McCollister Evarts lamented: "That old genteel existence [once the hallmark of academia] is gone, probably forever."

Clearly, it would take a strong team to succeed in this troublesome decade of the '90s. Once again, Dr. Bob's talent for "supporting talented people who are smarter than I am and getting out of their way" made for a successful transition to a model that ensured that academic medicine's traditional three-legged stool—education, research, patient care—had a strong, sound base. Fortunately, he was working with a seasoned team. Marshall Lichtman became the school's sixth dean and Paul Griner would continue as CEO of Strong Memorial Hospital.

This new leadership model, developed "in house" and adopted by President Dennis O'Brien and university trustees, would become a success due in large part to the strong, decades-long working relationships among Joynt, Griner, Lichtman, Robinson, and later Leo Brideau, who succeeded Griner as hospital COO. (As for the collegiality between Dr. Bob and the nursing school dean Sheila Ryan, well, "It's all in the Irish," as they say.) All four valued Bob's skill— and his good humor—in bringing together those with disparate views. Together they would promote and support all of the Medical Center's constituent parts.

That strong team was now in place. Let's see how well they fared.

❧   ❧   ❧

A strategic planning process began the decade, long hours of work that would result in major changes in organization, programs, outreach, and especially in planning for what would become a dramatic expansion of the Medical Center's physical presence between Crittenden Road and Elmwood Avenue. Space was desperately needed for both outpatient care and research; finding a solution and designing its implementation were high on the planning agenda. Outpatient care needs would be addressed with a large modern ambulatory care building attached to the hospital, facing east toward Mt. Hope Avenue. Next would come a four-storey research wing at the intersection of Elmwood and Lattimore Roads, with direct access to the medical school. In 1994, ground was broken for the ambulatory facility, including a parking garage, and planning was well underway for the research wing.

As Vice President Joynt dealt with the broader issues within the Medical Center, he never lost sight of the department that he had founded and chaired for so long. After a national search, one of his own trainees, Berch Griggs, was appointed chair of neurology. Dr. Griggs had learned well from Bob, and with support and encouragement from above he built on the talented faculty already in place, expanded the department's research, teaching, and clinical programs with new recruits, and led the department to international recognition for excellence.

The Medical Center's regional role was elevated with Strong Memorial Hospital's designation as a Level 1 Regional Trauma Center, and the first informal affiliations with other hospitals were developed in the Southern Tier and in Canandaigua and Batavia. The new vice president was deeply involved in developing these early partnerships, which paved the way for today's expanded affiliations, including that of Strong Memorial and Highland Hospital in 1995.

The early '90s saw the creation of specialized centers of excellence. By integrating disciplines and programs these centers of specialization brought together physicians, researchers, and caregivers mutually involved in similar issues. New partnerships would replace a "silo mentality" with one that encouraged idea sharing and implementation. "Centers of excellence" as a concept also proved to be an effective marketing tool, attracting new patients, research funding, faculty, and medical students.

New programs—including a $4.5 million federally funded Center on Aging, a $1 million AIDS research facilities program with a grant from the NIH, and a $2.9 million Robert Woods Johnson grant for educational change rooted in Rochester's biopsychosocial model—were formulated, funded, and implemented during these years. Emergency medicine became a department, as did biostatistics. A comprehensive epilepsy program was developed, and a new Department of Environmental Medicine brought together research and clinical faculty, with mercury, lead, and astronaut-performance studies among its components.

Of course, things did not always go smoothly. At the beginning of the decade, some clinical faculty were holding office-related accounts at local banks, with little or no transparency, a potentially contentious situation that had to be changed. It was. When new Dean Lichtman convened the faculty meeting to address this troublesome issue, he was presented with a mock suit of armor by the chair of the medical faculty council, a gift to make clear that Dr. Bob's way of defusing a situation with humor was still alive and well.

Whereas most problems could be solved somewhere along the leadership chain, others required a final decision by the vice president himself. From Peter Robinson: "On one occasion, a major change had to be made high on the faculty roster. Bob was very reluctant to do this, it turned him inside out—but he never shied from doing the right thing. If you're not empathetic, it's easier to be political and decisive. Bob was none of that. He always tried to be careful not to cause more hurt than he needed to."

By the end of 1995, the effects of nearly catastrophic illness led to Dr. Bob's retirement from the vice presidential office, but not from the medical school, where he continued to be a mentor, teacher, adviser, and treasured presence. It had been, all in all, a vibrant half decade, one that saw enormous strides being taken, advances that would lead an energized Medical Center community toward the new millennium.

❧   ❧   ❧

A career steeped in recognition and honors reached its climax in 1992 with the *Festschrift* held in Dr. Bob's honor. This academic power event was, indeed, "the celebration of a lifetime."[5] That October, UR graduates traveled from across the country for the annual alumni weekend. Whatever their current occupation—business, arts, medicine, history, or music—they crowded into Rochester's Crown Plaza Hotel for the Saturday night banquet featuring as guest speaker the honoree himself—the renowned crowd pleaser par excellence.

But for those in healthcare, the heart of the weekend was the two-day *Festschrift* held at the Medical Center that brought together a distinguished array of medical scientists to honor Dr. Bob. The colloquium highlighted two areas in which Dr. Bob was internationally known: Alzheimer's disease and the ethics of medical journalism. Adding a special *frisson* to the discussion of the latter was the presence of the two key speakers, the editor of the *Journal of American Medicine* (*JAMA*) and the editor of the *New England Journal of Medicine*, who at that moment were publicly disagreeing on a current issue.

The convening of a *Festschrift* is a clear indication that an academic legacy has been achieved. Dr. Bob's legacy is, indeed, one to be remembered—and it was secured, finally and firmly, during his years as vice president for health affairs. That Saturday evening of alumni weekend 1992 at the Crown Plaza, Dr. Bob was again at his Irish best, face shining and smiling, greeting friends and trainees from across the country and around the world, filling everyone with good cheer—and pride in being part of the University of Rochester family.

DR. BOB'S "DARK DAYS"

The trouble began after a cross-country airplane trip in 1993. A week of feeling "not quite right" followed. There was occasional coughing, not unusual after a plane trip—and hadn't he been coughing *before* they left for California? Breathing became more difficult. And then, suddenly, things got worse, so bad that Margaret called the family's internist Dr. Raymond Mayewski at Strong Memorial Hospital: "Ray, something is really wrong. Bob's not breathing well, he's weak, and his color's off." "Bring him right in. I'll meet you in Emergency," said Mayewski.

One look at the patient made the situation clear: "Margaret, Bob's not oxygenating, he has to be intubated." Test results were shocking: temperature above forty degrees, oxygen was barely forty and falling, platelet count below forty thousand, CPK level well over forty thousand.[1] Doctors will understand those dire numbers. "Bob belonged to the 'Forty-Forty-Forty-Forty Club,'" Mayewski said later. "He may be its only member."

The patient, fitted with a breathing tube and sedated, failed to respond to any of the drugs that Mayewski ordered, all those medications that might have a chance of changing what seemed like a fatal outcome. "His lungs 'whited out,'" Mayewski recalls, "and we had no idea what was causing the problem. I knew that taking an open biopsy would probably kill him."

The situation worsened. Dr. Bob (now Vice-Provost Bob) lost his kidney function and dialysis was begun. His blood pressure dropped and his temperature continued to rise. Most alarming was his oxygen pressure, which had slipped into the forties. The neurologist Richard Moxley, a muscle specialist and a key member of Dr. Bob's own faculty team, had been following the case daily. Under Moxley and Mayewski's supervision, and to help the patient's body and brain absorb oxygen, Dr. Bob was deliberately paralyzed, using a curare-like medication. "The only thing that was keeping him alive was his heart," said Mayewski later—the same heart that had given him twinges of predictable, nonaccelerated angina for almost eighteen years. He would remain in the coma for four weeks, and for two months in Strong's Intensive Care Unit. Michelle Bonyak, for thirty years the ICU's nurse supervisor, brought all her remarkable nursing skills to Dr. Bob's bedside.

Perhaps also helping Dr. Bob through this trial were the prayers and good wishes of hundreds of well-wishers from the Medical Center and university community, friends throughout the city and suburbs, and faculty and former medical residents from across the country. "How's Bob Joynt doing?" was a spoken concern that resonated throughout that year, and well after. Most faithful of all, of course, were Margaret and the Joynt sons and daughters. Throughout the long days and weeks, they talked to their dearly beloved, talked about anything that might light a spark, hoping, praying, over the unresponsive body lying in the hospital bed.

When Dr. Bob finally surfaced from his deep coma, his eyelids were the only parts of his body that he could move. Single-syllable communication would come slowly. One day, aware that Mayewski was in the room, he motioned the doctor to his bedside and then whispered his first full sentence: "Ray, don't screw this up!" "We're doing our best, Bob," Mayewski told him—and they certainly were. Finally, many days later, Mayewski gave Bob's daughter Kathy Joynt the good news: "Your father is no longer the sickest person in this hospital."

Dr. Bob had survived, although the reasons for his near-death experience and his unofficial enrollment as a member of the "Forty-Forty-Forty-Forty Club," are still unclear. Then began a long year of rehab, including two months in Strong Memorial's rehab unit, his slow, painful progress supervised by the unit chief Dr. Charles Gibson. At first, a mechanized lift raised Dr. Bob's limp body into a chair where he could do simple arm and leg exercises. Eventually, he could stand, holding on to support bars; after thirty days, he walked thirty steps. His daughters stood by, crying with joy.

Fortunately, Dr. Bob's extraordinary mind—and his determination—had not been affected. That summer, he continued to recuperate at the family cottage on Keuka Lake, taking physical therapy in the nearby village of Penn Yan. A year later, he could walk normally. "Bob was an easy fellow to take care of," Dr.

Mayewski says. "He'd had three strikes, but he wasn't out. Once recovered, he would come in, sit down, and be very clear about the issues and problems."

"It's hard to separate Bob from his family," says Mayewski. "I loved to make home visits, sitting in his living room. One year around Christmas time, after that terrible illness had ended, I heard a knock on my door. There on the porch were the six Joynt sons and daughters, singing Christmas carols. Each of them handed me a gift—and each one thanked me for saving their father."

❧   ❧   ❧

Everyone who knew Dr. Bob remembers him as a brilliant, kind, compassionate, and funny man, a man more interested in other people than in himself. What's often forgotten is how much he endured during his last years while remaining a continuing force for good at the Medical Center. A series of physical setbacks, several of them major, were often disguised by a nature that seemed incurably optimistic. "NBD," he would tell Margaret—"No big deal."

In fact, the years following "the dark days" of 1993 presented Dr. Bob with trials that call to mind the biblical Job. In 1996, a retinal vein occlusion damaged his only good eye. With his vision ever weaker and no longer able to drive, he continued to play golf, although often his golf partners had to find the ball for him.[2] There were other setbacks: a big toe lost to gangrene, infection in a transplanted leg vein, the stress of a cardiac bypass operation, and melanoma of the ear followed by reconstructive surgery. All crises were successfully resolved, thanks to skilled medical care, but all took their toll.

In spite of these setbacks, during the early days of this millennium, Dr. Bob's short, solid, white-coated figure could be seen making its way through the halls of the Medical Center, often accompanied by a retinue of eager residents. His grand rounds presentations were fewer now, but they were always packed. Each burst of laughter suggested that Dr. Bob was continuing to use humor to pass along the humanistic values that were so integral to the man himself. A new generation of physicians was being imbued by the legendary Joynt spirit.

LIFE WITH FATHER

In 1947, in a rush of postwar high spirits, Americans flocked to see a Technicolor comedy about a family of red-headed boys and their long-suffering mother living in a household with a stubborn, grumpy father. (Yes, *Life with Father* really *was* a comedy.)[1]

Bob Joynt was as different from Clarence Day, the father in the Lindsay and Crouse crowd-pleaser, as black is to white, night to day. Anything but stubborn and ill-natured, the head of the Joynt household—wife, six lively offspring, and for a while a beloved mother-in-law—led a family whose action-packed, laughter-filled life is a story in itself. Skiing, sailing, traveling, playing, feasting, laughing, joking, visiting, storytelling, fathering, husbanding—all this was frosting on the cake of a professional life extraordinarily complex and demanding.

"The adjective I would use to describe both my parents is 'convivial,'" says Robert J. Joynt III.[2] "Dad had a very busy professional life, but he was always a big presence in our everyday lives." The thousands of friends and colleagues who have experienced the Joynt conviviality would agree.

Throughout all the family's varied activities runs a lightness of spirit that started early and lasted long. It began for the children, perhaps, with the nightly bedtime ritual. A story, often about the mischievous "Willie McKeever" (Dad's creation) was followed by father leading a parade of children up the stairs while chanting "Boom-dee-boom, dee-biddley-boom," a call enthusiastically echoed by his fledglings.

Daughter Anne Joynt[3] describes her Dad's days off at home, a routine that began early in the morning with him wrestling with the on-line version of the *New York Times* crossword puzzle—and winning. "I would just be getting up when he would announce, 'I think you will find that the puzzle was completed this morning in twenty-three minutes,'" she recalls. "Then off he would go, carrying a cup of coffee to the love of his life, our mother. Inevitably the uniform of the day would be the ubiquitous J. C. Penney white, short-sleeved shirt and L. L. Bean khaki pants." His favorite breakfast would include such questionable food groups as kippers, scrapple, or chipped beef on toast, the latter familiar (under a different, all-initial name) from his days in the army.

We learn from Anne that her dad seemed nowhere happier than at the head of the family table, telling jokes and stories, and "asking us what new words we had learned that day." She knows what her father *didn't* like: green vegetables, sad movies, the Dallas Cowboys, idle gossip, and the end of summer. What he *did* like was being Irish, linguini and clam sauce, grappa, "Edelweiss" and "Danny Boy," anything and everything from the state of Iowa, and oysters of every kind, shape, and place of origin "known or yet to be invented." What he loved above all was his family—and his work.

❧   ❧   ❧

Margaret Joynt points out that, as a busy father, Bob built strong connections with his children based on their individual interests. With first-born Bob it was a mutual fascination with math and science; with Tom,[4] sports (often extreme sports)—skiing, sailing, mountain climbing, and hammer-and-nails building projects. Kathy,[5] Mary,[6] and Trish[7] all at one time or another were involved in their father's editorial projects. Anne and Trish's artistic talents amazed Dr. Bob, who claimed he had none of his own.

Tom Joynt still appreciates how supportive his father was, not just to him, but to all his siblings, encouragement that perfectly matched each one's interest. "At Christmas, we could expect to get a book related to what we were involved with at the time. That's the way he learned too. When Dad took up skiing, I saw a whole pile of books about skiing on his bedside table."

Daughter Kathy describes her relationship with her father this way: "My pockets are full of the lovely times I had the privilege of sharing with my Dad: a morning walk down the lake road, reciting "The Lake Isle at Innisfree" together, playing—or rather being beat at—Scrabble, discussing his next editorial for *Neurology*, and talking about words."

❧   ❧   ❧

Family games were always important. Word games topped the list, and few in the family could match the senior Joynt's extraordinary skill and vast mental storehouse of often-exotic knowledge. (At the Medical Center, Dean Marshal Lichtman referred to him as "our Google.") Scrabble, crossword puzzles, alphabet games during long car trips—all raised the bar for the Joynt children, who learned to meet the test, and benefitted.

Chess was another matter. Dr. Bob, who had been taught the game by his uncle, joined the chess club at UI. While he was on the faculty there, multiple chess boards often were set up at the Joynts' home, and young Bobby was allowed to stay up late to watch the play. As a kindergartener, he was a competent player; at eight, he was beating schoolmates much older than he; and when he was in high school, his father was heard to say, "I don't mind being beaten by my son, but it's tough when Bobby is sitting with his back to the board—and doing his homework at the same time."[8]

And let's not forget the dancing! Bob *loved* to polka, and so did Margaret. Daughter Mary remembers how limber her father was in his younger days, and how the renowned neurologist could astonish friends with his prowess at the Russian Cossacks' dance, his body low to the ground and legs flung forward, left, then right, in rapid succession. Even "the Twist" had its moment, and, of course, there was often Irish dancing, at which both Anne and Mary became adept.

Perhaps it had something to do with dancing, but Bob Joynt was shoeless by choice as a child, shoeless at the lake, and shoeless at home. The pattern repeated itself for years and years. Mary Joynt Wodarski says, "I used to pretend my Dad's toes were piano keys—and I could almost always play, because when he was home, he never wore shoes." How's that for a world figure in academic medicine?

❧   ❧   ❧

For twenty years, summer for the Joynts was synonymous with freedom. And freedom meant two (occasionally three) weeks at a lake in northern Minnesota, where a resort community of simple log cottages became a precious and unforgettable part of their lives, starting from the moment that eight Joynts of varying ages piled into the family station wagon, the ignition key was turned, and the two-day drive to their destination began. (For the children, even the two nights spent at the same hotels with swimming pool was a treat to be relished, a double pleasure repeated on the trip back home.)

The real joy began the morning after their arrival at the cottage, when all six fledglings shed their shoes for the rest of the summer and followed their father as he jumped into the lake for an early morning "dock dipper." Everyone learned to water ski at Leech Lake, a thrilling new pleasure. For Margaret, there was freedom from the kitchen, with delicious and plentiful meals served in the community lodge. Most days ended sweetly, toasting marshmallows and telling stories around the campfire, as tall, dark pines whispered above them.

For Dr. Bob, these weeks at the lake meant precious family time—and a much-needed respite from his multiple professional demands. Perhaps best of all was the prospect of hours he now could spend reading, savoring the stack of books, his essential luggage, that had been packed away in the station wagon back on Sandpiper Lane in Pittsford.

❧   ❧   ❧

Kenneth Graham in his classic tale *The Wind in the Willows*, always a favorite bedtime story for the young Joynts, made one thing very clear: "There is nothing—absolutely nothing—half so much worth doing as simply messing about in boats." As man and boy, Bob Joynt could not have agreed more.

Whether it was lazying around Iowa's Lake Okoboji as a boy, vacationing with his parents and sisters' families, silently paddling a kayak through the morning mists on Keuka Lake, or battling wind, rain, and high seas on a sailboat off the coast of Maine, time spent on a boat, whatever its size and wherever the water, was for Bob Joynt time joyously spent.

Bob's sailing adventures turned international when, in the '60s, he was invited to join a group of serious sailors[9] marshaled by Rochester vascular surgeon Ethan Welch. After an initial cruise on Chesapeake Bay, Bob joined the group—as often as he could—on their annual yachting adventures, exploring American waters and European seas in alternate years. Later, sons, grandsons, and sons-in-law would complete the crew of what became known as "the Joynt boat." Traveling in a fleet of six or eight vessels, the friends sailed through seas as diverse as those around Turkey, Ireland, Corsica, the Caribbean, Mallorca, even Bora-Bora in the South Pacific. As Dr. Welch recalls: "Most of us brought with us a pile of high-tech gear [and other impedimenta]. Bob brought a little bag with a single change of clothes, some toiletries . . . and books." Of course.

Splendid and exciting these trips were, bonding friends forever. One day, after snorkeling in the coral reefs around Bora-Bora, Bob called "Commodore Welch" aside and said, "Ethan, I'm so grateful to you. You've changed my life. You've shown me a world I never would have known." But one would like to think that Bob's heart remained faithful to his forty-year-old sailboat, the sturdy craft that carried him time and again over the lovely and ancient waters of his favorite among New York's Finger Lakes, his beloved Keuka.

?? ?? ??

During his internship in Montreal, Dr. Bob had yearned to ski, but as he saw throngs of injured skiers brought into the hospital throughout the winter, he changed his mind. It wasn't until his son Tom took to the slopes with a competitive vengeance that both Bob and Margaret moved into support mode. Soon that meant loading eight pairs of skis on top of the station wagon and heading for the slopes. Every snowy weekend for several winters, Team Joynt would be on the road, either to one of Tom's races or for family skiing in the Bristol Hills or the Adirondacks.

Dr. Bob approached learning to ski with the same laser focus he seems to have applied to all situations. A friend once watched Bob grab a sandwich, hurry through lunch at the lodge, and then rush back to the ski lift for several more practice runs, while others lingered, chatting around the warm glow of barbecue fires. Skiing continued to be part of Bob and Margaret's lives even after the children had left home, as they joined groups of compatible friends for weekends at ski resorts in New York and New England. Building friends for a lifetime, wherever they happened to be, marked all the family's adventures.

?? ?? ??

In Lindsey and Crouse's comedy *Life with Father*, it was Mrs. Clarence Day who provided the glue that held the family together.

Within the Joynt family, the strong bonding was forged *equally* by both Bob and Margaret. But anyone who has ever met Margaret, or talked about her with Dr. Bob and their children, knows how central she has been both to his career and to the family's success as a thriving—and growing—community.

Bob and Margaret's partnership began when they were in college, she in Chicago, he in medical school at the University of Iowa. They postponed marrying until Dr. Bob had completed his Montreal internship and Margaret had received her law degree at the University of Iowa. Then, as newlyweds, they left for Cambridge and his fellowship year at the physiology laboratory at Cambridge University. There the great adventure really began.

"For fifty-eight years of our married life we were wedded in a deep mutual caring for each other, with a fervent desire that the other be happy," says Margaret. "That life was enriched by family, friends, our reading, and our many travels." Now in her Pittsford home, still surrounded by family and friends, her calendar is filled with a round of activities that combine all her many civic, social, political, and religious interests. Margaret's open heart and her interest in others make her a focus of friendship for hundreds of people. In a lonely apartment in London, Bob once scribbled in a makeshift journal, "I miss Margaret terribly. . . ." One can see why. Her energy equals his, her commitment to both family and community is powerful—and her eagerness to engage fully in life seems unquenchable.

That energy was continually being tapped. Throughout Dr. Bob's career, Margaret was the principal in a devoted support team—medical faculty and staff, family, and close friends—that stood ready to back up this man who was shouldering so many layers of responsibility. At home, Margaret cultivated a convivial atmosphere that drew people together. She orchestrated countless "at home" suppers for first-year medical and graduate students, serving friendship, conversation, and food cooked by her and served under a backyard tent. When department funds were tight, potential faculty recruits were entertained not at one of Rochester's fine restaurants, but at the Joynts' dinner table. Until Dr. Bob became dean, the Department of Neurology's annual Saturday-night-before-Christmas party was held "at home with the Joynts," lively gatherings that eventually included, as faculty numbers grew, seventy-five husbands, wives, and partners.

A good time always was had by all. (Just ask any of the Joynt off-spring who handled the clean-up evidence the morning after!)

For both Bob and Margaret, raising six bright, spirited, and independent offspring must have brought moments when the future seemed uncertain. (Has there ever been a life with no tears?) A challenge for the whole family arose in the mid-70s when Trish, then studying at the Rhode Island School of Design, began to experience the first signs of a neurological disorder. Four years later came the diagnosis—multiple sclerosis, surely the blackest of ironies for the renowned neurologist. Trish says, "My father knew all along [what the diagnosis would be]. I'm sure it was much harder on him and my mother than it was for me." Some career plans had to be limited, but Trish's indomitable spirit never flagged. Two gifts have helped her meet the challenges of living with MS, she says—marriage and the birth of a beloved daughter.

Bob often said, "I have eleven children—six sired and five acquired." The spouses chosen by the Joynts' sons and daughters are cherished. Now nine grandchildren bring lots of laughter to family gatherings, and their numbers continue to grow.

❧   ❧   ❧

In 1976, while raising six children through times of radical social change, Margaret spent six weeks cramming for the New York State Bar exam; Bob helped by shouldering many of the household responsibilities during those weeks. In September of that year when all America was celebrating the Bicentennial, Margaret began practicing as a law guardian for children before Monroe County's Family Court and Supreme Court.

By 1982, with the young Joynts now living away from home, Margaret and Bob could spend more time together, much of it traveling. As wife of a celebrated after-dinner speaker, several evenings every week were spent dining out. Often Margaret accompanied Bob around the country when he was guest lecturer at a university or serving as president of the three major neurological societies. For husband and wife, there were, in all, thirty trips abroad, including ten cherished annual trips to London. They traveled together to international neurology meetings and to London on sabbatical, they reconvened in Ireland and Italy with other wives after their sailor husbands' week at sea, they went on cruises with Dr. Bob's sisters. Whatever the destination, there were always new things to learn, new friends to meet, and pleasures to be enjoyed.

ॐ   ॐ   ॐ

Perhaps the best picture of Margaret McGivern Joynt comes from Dr. Bob himself, in a letter written in 1996 in honor of her birthday. With her permission, we share parts of that loving message with you.

> Dearest Margaret,
>
> I remember that night in December 1949 as clearly now as I did then . . . you came down the steps and caught my eye and never let it go. I thought you were the most beautiful, vivacious, captivating person I ever met—but every day you are even more so. . . . I know if you are late you are doing something for someone else, or if the toys are all over the house I know that all the kids on the block want to play at our house, or if the dishes aren't done you are playing with the kids (and now our grandkids). You have your priorities straighter than anyone I know. . . . I have some regrets for some of the decisions I made. But the decision to marry you made on that night in December 1949 becomes better every day of my life.
>
> All my love, Bob.

One last picture, this time of team Joynt in action, comes from the child neurologist Richard Moxley, who joined the Department of Neurology in 1974. Now a senior faculty member, Dr. Moxley leaves us this vivid memory of his welcome to Rochester: "Bob and Margaret took me and my family under their wing. They helped us settle in. It was so enjoyable to be part of the Joynt get-togethers, to meet their children, to do a little Irish dancing in their family room. I was a young man then, and Bob came to seem like a senior member of my own family, someone who watched over me while I was away from my own parents. A deep concern for others' welfare was how he ran his life and how he ran the Department of Neurology."

Many others at the Medical Center, both old-timers and more recent graduates, could share similar stories. This chapter of the

Bob Joynt story began with an intimate picture of life at home with the Joynts. But equally important is this: their concept of "family" was always democratic—the view was seen through a lens that always was wide open, inclusive, and panoramic.

Their remarkable partnership will be long remembered.

18

THE MAN OF FAITH

"Bob, do you still go to Mass?" asked an old friend, Joe Foley, long retired, during a late-in-life phone conversation. The answer: "Well, Joe, I made that commitment long ago—and I'm not going to go back on it now."

All his life, Bob Joynt was deeply, quietly devout. There was no religiosity about him, no excessive display of devotion. After all, this was the man who wanted you to know that Jesus actually was Irish. If you doubted, he'd explain, using his most Irish voice: "Just think of it—he's thirty-three years old, not married, has no job, lives with his parents . . ." (Even a nun would smile, if she were Irish.)

Yet this is the same man who would scour the phone book while traveling, searching for the closest church where he could attend Sunday Mass. *He* did this, the boy who went to public schools, not his wife, parochial-schooled Margaret. As an altar boy, he had promised to go to Mass every Sunday; as an adult, he was faithful in keeping that promise. For Robert Joynt, a promise made was a promise kept. (Perhaps especially important in this case, considering the possible consequences.)

"I have the sense that there was a single core in Bob Joynt, a profound unity of the personal, the professional, the spiritual, and the comic," says his friend Dennis O'Brien, former president of the University of Rochester and a noted philosopher. "Being human is a comic mystery. Such high ideals, such lame behavior—that's us. Bob could see that as a clinician and signal it with wry humor."

Dr. O'Brien believes that religion can provide the longest possible view, a faith in the future that can be especially helpful to those, like Dr. Bob, whose profession each day brings them face to face with pain, suffering, and every other issue related to human mortality. Pope Francis's charge—"The function of the church is to be a field hospital for the suffering"—seems appropriate in talking about Dr. Bob's life in medicine, O'Brien says.

Father Daniel Tormey knew Dr. Bob as both a friend and sailing companion. He also knows the world—as a priest, a prison chaplain, at Strong Memorial Hospital and the medical school, or while serving the church in Brazil or Belgium. "Faith was the bedrock foundation for both Bob's scientific mind and his compassionate heart," says Father Dan. "The way he could mesh the neurological and the theological was impressive. But as a priest, I believe his own goal was to become more perfectly human, because it's in our humanity that holiness is."

Though never a proselytizer, Bob Joynt never stopped honoring those rituals of the faith that were important to him. He'd asked Father Dan to be with him each time he faced surgery—heart, leg, eyes, ear—and the church's sacraments provided support and comfort to both patient and family.

Sailing one summer off the Maine coast in company with others, Bob asked Father Dan if he would say Mass on Sunday. Of course the priest agreed, expecting to serve three or four men, shipboard. On the appointed morning, he was surprised to see seven or eight dinghies full of sailors, men of differing faiths, their boats roped together, bobbing on the waves next to "the Commodore's" boat. "It was Bob's quiet inspiration and example that brought them together," the priest says. "That's just the way he was."

"I want to work till I die," Dr. Joynt often said. His wish was answered on the morning of April 13, 2012, when his heart—the motor that had been coaxed through several emergencies—finally stopped. He had just stepped into a Medical Center elevator on his way to grand rounds when he suddenly reached for the handrail, dropped to his knees, and closed his eyes.[1] All efforts to revive him were unsuccessful.

In his eulogy a few weeks later, Father Dan spoke to an overflow crowd at Pittsford's Church of the Transfiguration, reminding them of what most of them already knew, but wanted to hear again. "Dr. Joynt knew the map of the human mind as few do," he told them. "He knew the path of human behavior—and the obstacles that prevent us from being human. He knew the beautiful, the funny, the artistic. He knew friendship . . . and love in all its shades and degrees. He knew that the human spirit is always seeking more, and he never retired from the search."

A few days before he died, Dr. Bob was asked, once again, whether he believed in an afterlife. With a familiar, reassuring grin, he thrust both thumbs skyward and responded, "I'm countin' on it!" Amen.

➤   ➤   ➤

In 2013, the first annual Dr. Robert J. Joynt Jr. Kindness Award was presented at the Medical Center's honors ceremony. The threefold award honors a doctor, nurse, and staff person who best exemplify the words by which Dr. Joynt is best known: "You can't always be right, but you can always be kind."

APPENDIX

Curriculum Vitae

Owing to space limitations, abstracts, medical school consultancies, and medical school committees are not included in this shortened version. The complete CV is listed online at https://www.urmc.rochester.edu/MediaLibraries/URMCMedia/neurology/documents/Robert_Joynt_cv.pdf.

Robert J. Joynt, MD, PhD

Address: Department of Neurology
            University of Rochester School of Medicine and Dentistry
            601 Elmwood Avenue, Box 673
            Rochester, NY 14642

Birthplace: Le Mars, Iowa

Date of Birth: December 22, 1925

Family: Married: Wife, Margaret McGivern
Children: Robert, Patricia, Mary, Anne, Thomas, and Kathleen
Military Service: Staff Sergeant, US Army Signal Corps, 1944–46

Education

1964   DSc (Honorary), Westmar College, Le Mars, Iowa
1963   PhD, Anatomy, University of Iowa
1963   MS, Anatomy, University of Iowa
1952   MD, University of Iowa, Iowa City, Iowa
1949   BA, Westmar College, Le Mars, Iowa

Professional History

1952–53   Intern, Royal Victoria Hospital, Montreal, Canada

1953–54	Postgraduate researcher, Department of Physiology, Cambridge, England
1954–57	Resident, Department of Neurology, University Hospital, Iowa City, IA
1954–57	Fellow, USPHS, Department of Neurology, University of Iowa College of Medicine, Iowa City, IA
1957	Staff, Intermediate Grade, Veterans Administration Hospital, Iowa City, IA
1957–58	Associate, Department of Neurology, University of Iowa College of Medicine, Iowa City, IA
1957–66	Attending Physician, Veterans Hospital, Iowa City, IA
1957–66	Attending Staff, Department of Neurology, University Hospitals, Iowa City, IA
1958–59	Acting Director, Division of Electroencephalography, University Hospitals, Iowa City, IA
1961–66	Assistant Professor, Department of Neurology, University of Iowa, Iowa City, IA
1966–84	Neurologist-in-Chief, Department of Neurology, Strong Memorial Hospital, Rochester, NY
1966–84	Chairman, Department of Neurology, University of Rochester, Rochester, NY
1966–2012	Professor of Neurology, University of Rochester, Rochester, NY
1966–2012	Professor of Neurobiology and Anatomy, University of Rochester, Rochester, NY
1968–72	Director, History of Medicine, University of Rochester, Rochester, NY
1968–85	Consultant, Genesee Hospital, Rochester, NY
1969–85	Consultant, Rochester General Hospital, Rochester, NY
1975–2002	Consultant, Highland Hospital, Rochester, NY
1977–90	Consultant (Civilian), US Air Force
1979–90	Consultant, Monroe Community Hospital, Rochester, NY
1981–86	Edward A. and Alma Vollertson Rykenboer Professor of Neurophysiology, University of Rochester, Rochester, NY
1984–85	Acting Dean, University of Rochester School of Medicine and Dentistry, Rochester, NY
1985–89	Dean, University of Rochester School of Medicine and Dentistry, Rochester, NY
1985–94	Vice Provost for Health Affairs, University of Rochester, Rochester, NY
1989–94	Vice President for Health Affairs, University of Rochester, Rochester, NY

1997–2012 Distinguished University Professor, Provost's Office, University of Rochester, Rochester, NY
2002–4 Attending with Admit, Department of Neurology, Strong Memorial Hospital, Rochester, NY

Awards and Honors

1949 Graduated BA, magna cum laude, Westmar College, Le Mars, IA
1951 Alpha Omega Alpha, University of Iowa, Iowa City, IA
1952 Murchison MacEwen Prize (outstanding graduate student), University of Iowa College of Medicine
1952 Omicron Delta Kappa, University of Iowa, Iowa City, IA
1964 DSc (Honorary), Westmar College, Le Mars, IA
1970 Distinguished Alumni Award, University of Iowa College of Medicine Centennial, Iowa City, IA
1980 Fogarty Senior International Fellow, NIH, Bethesda, MD
1982 Herbert W. Mapstone Award for Excellence in Teaching, University of Rochester, Rochester, NY
1984 Award of Merit, Rochester Academy of Medicine, Rochester, NY
1985 Gold-Headed Cane Award, University of California, San Francisco, CA
1987 Robert J. Joynt Award for Excellence in Neurology (est. University of Iowa as annual award), Iowa City, IA
1988 Frank H. Netter, MD Award, American Academy of Neurology, Minneapolis, MN
1989 E. Mott Moore Award, Monroe County Medical Society, Rochester, NY
1989 Gold Medal Award, Medical Alumni Association, University of Rochester, Rochester, NY
1989 The Robert J. Joynt Lecture sponsored by Physicians for Social Responsibility, University of Rochester, Rochester, NY
1990 A. B. Baker Award for Lifetime Achievement in Neurology, American Academy of Neurology, Minneapolis, MN
1991 T. Franklin Williams Foundation Award, Rochester, NY
1991 Ellen Browning Scripps Society Medal, The Ellen Browning Scripps Society, Scripps Memorial Hospitals Foundation, La Jolla, CA
1991 Edward C. Yoder Award, Saint Joseph Hospital and Health Care Center, Tacoma, WA

1992	The George W. Jacoby Award, American Neurological Association Annual Meeting, Toronto, Canada
1992	Robert J. Joynt Prize for Excellence in Clinical Neurology, University of Rochester, Rochester, NY
1993	The Albert David Kaiser Medal, Rochester Academy of Medicine, Rochester, NY
1995	Lifetime Achievement Award, Arthritis Foundation Local Chapter, Rochester, NY
1996	Honoree, The American Heart Association, Rochester, NY
1996	Fellow, American Association for the Advancement of Science, Washington, DC
1997	Distinguished University Professor, University of Rochester, Rochester, NY
1997	University of Iowa College of Medicine Distinguished Alumni Award for Achievement, Iowa City, IA
2011	Neurology Senior Faculty Award, Department of Neurology, University of Rochester School of Medicine and Dentistry, Rochester, NY
2011	Robert J. Joynt Chair Professorship in Experimental Therapeutics in Neurology, Department of Neurology, University of Rochester, Rochester, NY

Honorary Lecturer

1969	Penfield Lecturer, American University of Beirut, Beirut, Lebanon
1972	Dent Lecturer, Dent Neurologic Institute and State University of New York, Buffalo, NY
1975	Stevens Lecturer, University of Colorado, Boulder, CO
1978	Baker Lecturer, University of Minnesota, Minneapolis, MN
1979	Alpha Omega Alpha Lecturer, University of Iowa, Iowa City, IA
1980	Benjamin Boshes Lecturer and Professor, Northwestern University, Chicago, IL
1980	Jacobson Lecturer, Newcastle University, Newcastle-upon-Tyne, England
1980	Annual Neuroscience Lecture, Louisiana State University, New Orleans, LA
1980	Distinguished Guest Lecturer, University of Nebraska, Lincoln, NE
1980	Robert Aird Lecturer and Professor, University of California, San Francisco, CA

1980	Distinguished Lecturer, American College of Physicians, Dallas, TX
1981	Richard M. Paddison Scholar and Lecturer, Louisiana State University, New Orleans, LA
1981	Joseph Gitt Lecture, Washington University, St. Louis, MO
1984	David Seegal Alpha Omega Alpha Professor and Lecturer, Columbia University, NY
1984	The Himelfarb Lecture, Sinai Hospital, Baltimore, MD
1985	Jerome Merlis Lecturer, University of Maryland, Baltimore, MD
1985	William J. Kerr Gold-Headed Cane Lecturer, University of California, San Francisco, CA
1985	Norman Geschwind Memorial Lecture, Behavioral Neurology Society, Dallas, TX
1987	Alpha Omega Alpha Professor and Lecturer, The Ohio State University, Columbus, OH
1987	Joseph M. Foley Lecture, Case Western Reserve, Cleveland, OH
1987	Investiture Lecturer, West Virginia School of Medicine, Morgantown, WV
1988	Netter Lecture, American Academy of Neurology, Cincinnati, OH
1988	Dent Lecture, State University of New York (Buffalo), Buffalo, NY
1988	Clay Dinc Memorial Lecture, High Plains Baptist Hospital, Amarillo, TX
1989	History of Health Sciences Lecture Series, University of Virginia, Charlottesville, VA
1989	William Root Lecturer, Aloha Omega Alpha, University of Kansas School of Medicine, Kansas City, KS
1990	Alvin L. Ureles Lecture, The Genesee Hospital, Rochester, NY
1990	The Levy-Moskowitz Lecture, Morgan-Rochester Conference, Rochester, NY
1991	Pulsifer Lecture, Rochester Academy of Medicine, Rochester, NY
1991	The Ellen Browning Scripps Society Lecture, Scripps Memorial Hospitals Foundation, La Jolla, CA
1991	The Edwin C. Yoder Honor Lectures, Saint Joseph Hospital and Healthcare Center, Tacoma, WA
1992	Maurice W. Van Allen Lecture, University of Iowa College of Medicine, Iowa City, IA

1992	Jacoby Lecture, American Neurological Association, Mount Laurel, NJ
1993	Alpha Omega Alpha Visiting Professor and Lecturer, Pennsylvania State University College of Medicine, Hershey, PA
1995	Alpha Omega Alpha Lecturer, The Ohio State University, Columbus, OH
1999	Courville Lecturer, Loma Linda University Medical Center, Loma Linda, CA
1999	Taylor Lecture in Neuropsychiatry, University of Maryland, Baltimore, MD
2004	Leslie G. Rude Memorial Lecture, Hartwick College, Oneonta, NY

Editorial Appointments

1964–74	Board of Editors, *Medical Digest*
1966–84	Board of Editors, *Cortex*
1972–80	Advisory Board, Clinical Neurology Information Center
1973	Board of Editors, *Perspectives in Biology and Medicine*
1973–76	Board of Editors, *Neurology*
1973–84	Board of Editors, *Brain and Language*
1974–75	Editorial Advisory Committee for Clinical Neuroscience Section for the Twenty-Fifth Anniversary of *NINDS*
1975–79	Board of Editors, Reference and Index Service
1980–82	Associate Editor, *Archives of Neurology*
1980–85	Chief Editor, *Seminars of Neurology*
1982–97	Chief Editor, *Archives of Neurology*
1982	Board of Editors, *JAMA*
1984	Editor, *Advances in Applied Neurological Sciences* (Heidelberg, West Germany: Springer-Verlag)
1985	Founding Editor, *Seminars of Neurology*
1987–90	Board of Editors, *Archives of Gerontology and Geriatrics*
1988–89	Editorial Advisory Board, ISI *Atlas of Science*
1992–96	Member, Board of Regents, National Library of Medicine
1993	Member, Editorial Board, Continuum, American Academy of Neurology
1998	Newsletter Editor, "Changes + People + Comments," *Neurology*, official journal of the American Academy of Neurology

Organizations

1954	Royal Society of Medicine
1955	American Medical Association
1955–66	Iowa State Medical Society
1965–66	Johnson County Medical Society (Secretary-Treasurer)
1966–85	New York State Medical Society (Chairman, Section on History of Medicine; 1968–75, Vice Chairman, Section on Neurology, 1976–77; Member, Committee on Medical School Relations, 1985)
1955	American Academy of Neurology (Fellow, 1962–2012; Chairman, Nominating Committee, 1967; Chairman, Silas Weir Mitchell Committee, 1967–68; Publications Committee, 1967; Program Chairman, 1969–73; Board of Governors, 1971; President-elect, 1975–77; President, 1977–79; Special Courses Committee, 1979–81; Long-Range Planning Committee, 1982–84; Delegate for Neural Sciences, 1985; Bylaws Committee, 1987–89; Long-Range Planning Committee, 1987–89; Delegate to Royal Society of Medicine, 1987–89; Nominations Committee, 1989–91; Royal Society of Medicine Representative, 1989–91; Chair, Search Committee for Editor of *Neurology*, 1995; Honorary Member, 1997)
1957–66	Central EEG Society
1958–74	American Epilepsy League
1963	American EEG Society (Program Chairman, 1963; Membership Committee, 1964–66; Councilor, 1967–69; Rules Committee, 1967–69; Training Committee, 1976–77)
1958–90	Association for Research in Nervous and Mental Diseases
1959	American College of Physicians (Fellow, 1964)
1959–67	American Association for the History of Medicine; AAHM Rochester Local Arrangements Committee, 2005–2012
1960–66	Central Society for Neurological Research (Secretary Treasurer, 1963–65; President, 1965–66)
1963–80	American Association of Anatomists
1963–94	American Neurological Association (Councilor, 1967–69; Program Committee, 1979–82; Long-Range Planning Committee, 1983–85; Councilor, 1984; President-elect, 1986–87; President, 1987–88; Honorary Membership, 1991; Chairman, Advisory Committee for Honorary Membership, 1989–90; Chairman, Nominations Committee, 1990–91; Chairman of History Section, 1994)
1964–70	Society of Experimental Biology and Medicine

1966–80	Cajal Society (Association of University Professor of Neurology, 1969; Executive Committee, 1969–80)
1967–71	American Medical Association (Section on Psychiatry and Neurology, 1967–71; Assistant Secretary, 1967–69; Vice Chairman, 1969–71)
1967–76	Rochester Academy of Medicine, Section on Neurology (Chairman, 1967–69, Board of Governors, 1973–76)
1971–75	American Medical Association, Section on Neurology, Chairman
1973–76	American Board of Medical Specialties
1973–80	Director, American Board of Psychiatry and Neurology (Vice President, 1978; President, 1979)
1981–85	Member, Medical Advisory Board, Alzheimer's Disease Group of Rochester
1983	Director, People-to-People Tour (Neurology) to Europe
1984	Member, London Medical Society
1984–93	Rochester Area Hospital Association (Board 1984–89, Chairman, 1989–93)
1985–90	Member, New York Academy of Sciences
1985–90	Member, Council of Biology Editors
1987	Honorary Member, American Society for Neurological Investigation
1987–89	Member, New York State Council on Graduate Medical Education (Member, Subcommittee on the Development of Consortia)
1988–89	Rita G. Rudel Foundation, Board of Trustees
1988	Sight Savers International, Board of Directors
1989	Finger Lakes Health Systems Agency, Community Health Center Study Steering Committee
1995	Honorary Board Member, Children's Hospital at Strong

Visiting Professor or Invited Lecturer

Albany Medical Center
University of Buffalo
Dent Neurological Institute, Buffalo, NY
Montreal General Hospital
Montreal Neurologic Institute
Dartmouth Medical School
Boston Neurological Society
Boston University
University of Vermont
Upstate Medical Center, Syracuse, NY

Sayre Clinic, Sayre, PA
University of Pennsylvania
Cornell Medical School
Ithaca College
Mt. Sinai Medical School
Albert Einstein Medical School
University of Maryland
George Washington Medical School
Georgetown University
Bowman-Gray Medical School
Louisiana State University
University of Tennessee
University of Colorado
Washington University, St. Louis, MO
University of Kansas
University of Iowa
University of Minnesota
Case-Western Reserve, Cleveland, OH
University of Washington, Seattle
University of California, San Francisco
University of Arizona
University of New Mexico
Mayo Clinic, Rochester, MN
Beaumont Army Hospital, El Paso, TX
Lackland Air Force Base, San Antonio, TX
University of Texas, San Antonio
Letterman Army Hospital, San Francisco, CA
University of Massachusetts
Massachusetts General Hospital
University of Nebraska
University of Michigan
University of Oklahoma
University of Kentucky
New York Academy of Medicine
New York University School of Medicine
Northwestern University
Brown University
University of Texas, Dallas, TX
Columbia University
Harvard University
University of Aachen
Zurich University
University of Munich, Germany

Max Planck Institute, Munich, Germany
American University of Beirut, Lebanon
University of Wurzburg, Germany
University of Haifa, Israel
University of Lisbon, Portugal
Charing Cross Hospital, London, England
St. Mary's Hospital, London, England
St. Thomas's Hospital, London, England
London Hospital, London, England
Institute of Psychiatry, London, England
Queen Square, Institute of Neurology, London, England
King's College, London, England
Oxford University, Oxford, England
Newcastle University, Newcastle, England
London Medical Society, London, England
University of West Virginia
The Ohio State University
University of Western Ontario, London, Canada
University of Toronto, Toronto, Canada
University of Michigan, Ann Arbor
University of Wisconsin, Madison
Johns Hopkins Medical School, Baltimore, MD
Dartmouth College Medical School, Hanover, NH

Journal Articles:

Joynt, RJ. 2014. "The case of the locked house: The finished mystery." *Neurology* 83 (7): 661–64.
Joynt, RJ. 2013. "The case of the locked house: The unfinished mystery." *Neurology* 81 (11): 1018–19.
Joynt, RJ. 2011. "The silent witness and Charcot's hat." *Neurology* 76 (15): 1358–61.
Joynt, RJ. 2010. "And many more." *Archives of Neurology* 67 (6): 661.
Joynt, RJ. 2009. "The case of the misguided squire." *Neurology* 73 (2): 154–56.
Joynt, RJ. 2008. "The case of the collapsing man." *Neurology* 71 (9): 690–93.
Joynt, RJ. 2008. "The case of the colorless crystals" [letter]. *Neurology* 70 (13): 1055.
Joynt, RJ. 2007. "The case of the colorless crystals." *Neurology* 69 (9): 931–35.
Joynt, RJ. 2006. "The case of the reed in the breeze." *Neurology* 66 (11): 1782–84.

Joynt, RJ. 1998. "Changes + People + Comments." *Neurology* (serial column, 1998–2012).

Joynt, RJ. 1997. "Crisis in the presidency: The physician's role in assessing official capacity." *Neurology* 49 (5): 1208–9.

Joynt, RJ, and RM Kurlan. 1997. "Neurology." *JAMA* 277 (23): 1873–74.

Joynt, RJ. 1997. "Neurogenetics and primary care." *Neurology* 48 (1): 2–3.

Joynt, RJ. 1996. "The neurologist and managed care." *Archives of Neurology* 53 (9): 848.

Joynt, RJ. 1996. "Neurology." *JAMA* 275 (23): 1826–27.

Joynt, RJ. 1996. "The cost of strokes: Two views." *Neurology* 46 (3): 602.

Joynt, RJ. 1996. "Microbial threats." *Archives of Neurology* 53 (1): 17.

Joynt, RJ. 1995. "Neurology." *JAMA* 273 (21): 1695–97.

Joynt, RJ. 1994. "Neurology." *JAMA* 271 (21): 1686–87.

Joynt, RJ. 1994. "Who is minding the world?" *JAMA* 272 (21): 1699–700.

Joynt, RJ. 1993. "Neurology." *JAMA* 270 (2): 228–30.

Joynt, RJ. 1992. "Neurology." *JAMA* 268 (3): 380–82.

Joynt, RJ, JG Marshall, and LW McClure. 1991. "Financial threats to hospital libraries." *JAMA* 266 (9): 1219–20.

Joynt, RJ. 1991. "Neurology." *JAMA* 265 (23): 3134–35.

Joynt, RJ. 1991. "Freeze the ocean." *Archives of Neurology* 48 (5): 471.

Joynt, RJ. 1990. "Lucretia W. McClure: Medical Library Association President, 1990–1991." *Bulletin of the Medical Library Association* 78 (3): 320–21.

Joynt, RJ. 1990. "Neurology." *JAMA* 263 (19): 2660–61.

Joynt, RJ. 1989. "Neurology." *JAMA* 261 (19): 2859–60.

Joynt, RJ. 1988. "Vascular dementia: Too much, or too little?" *Archives of Neurology* 45 (7): 801.

Joynt, RJ, and DM Gas. 1987. "Neural transplants: Are we ready?" *Annals of Neurology* 22 (4): 455–56.

Joynt, RJ. 1987. "Dementia and technology." *Archives of Neurology* 44 (1): 20.

Streicher, HZ, and RJ Joynt. 1986. "HTLV-III/LAV and the monocyte/macrophage." *JAMA* 256 (17): 2390–91.

Gash, DM, MF Notter, SH Okawara, AL Kraus, and RJ Joynt. 1986. "Amitotic neuroblastoma cells used for neural implants in monkeys." *Science* 233 (4771): 1420–22.

Caine, ED, and RJ Joynt. 1986. "Neuropsychiatry . . . again." *Archives of Neurology* 43 (4): 325–27.

Joynt, RJ. 1985. "Cerebral dominance." *Archives of Neurology* 42 (5): 427.

Joynt, RJ. 1985. "Return to work after stroke." *JAMA* 253 (2): 249.

Joynt, RJ. 1984. "Landmark perspective: A new look at death." *JAMA* 252 (5): 680–82.

Joynt, RJ, and TH McNeill. 1984. "Neuropeptides in aging and dementia." *Peptides* 5 (suppl. 1): 269–74.

Joynt, RJ. 1984. "The language of dementia." *Advances in Neurology* 42: 65–69.

Joynt, RJ, and JH Feibel. 1982. "Stroke: Another view." *Perspectives in Biology and Medicine.* 26 (1): 116–26.

Feibel, JH, CA Baldwin, and RJ Joynt. 1981. "Catecholamine-associated refractory hypertension following acute intracranial hemorrhage: Control with propranolol." *Annals of Neurology* 9 (4): 340–43.

Joynt, RJ, JH Feibel, and CM Sladek. 1981. "Antidiuretic hormone levels in stroke patients." *Annals of Neurology* 9 (2): 182–84.

McNeill, TH, SJ Buell, LW Lapham, and RJ Joynt. 1981. "Morphology of hypothalamic magnocellular neurosecretory cells of the aging human brain." *Transactions of the American Neurological Association* 106: 61–64.

Joynt, RJ. 1981. "A note for interns and residents: A new law and advice on its circumvention." *Perspectives in Biology and Medicine* 25 (1): 144–47.

Sladek, CD, and RJ Joynt. 1980. "Role of angiotensin in the osmotic control of vasopressin release by the organ-cultured rat hypothalamo-neurohypophyseal system." *Endocrinology* 106 (1): 173–78.

Joynt, RJ. 1980. "W. R. Ingram: A student's appreciation." *Perspectives in Biology and Medicine* 24 (1): 57–60.

Rudick, RA, and RJ Joynt. 1980. "Normal pressure hydrocephalus: A treatable dementia." *Texas Medicine* 76 (12): 46–49.

Sladek, CD, and RJ Joynt. 1979. "Cholinergic involvement in osmotic control of vasopressin release by the organ-cultured rat hypothalamo-neurohypophyseal system." *Endocrinology* 105 (2): 367–71.

Sladek, CD, and RJ Joynt. 1979. "Characterization of cholinergic control of vasopressin release by the organ-cultured rat hypothalamo-neurohypophyseal system." *Endocrinology* 104 (3): 659–63.

Sladek, CD, and RJ Joynt. 1979. "Angiotensin stimulation of vasopressin release from the rat hypothalamo-neurohypophyseal system in organ culture." *Endocrinology* 104 (1): 148–53.

Joynt, RJ. 1979. "Presidential address." *Neurology* 29 (12): 1557–60.

Feibel, JH, CA Baldwin, and RJ Joynt. 1979. "Stress-induced refractory hypertension following acute cerebrovascular events: Control with propranolol." *Transactions of the American Neurological Association* 104: 138–41.

Shoulson, I, D Goldblatt, M Charlton, and RJ Joynt. 1978. "Huntington's disease: Treatment with muscimol, a GABA-mimetic drug." *Annals of Neurology* 4 (3): 279–84.

Sladek, CD, and RJ Joynt. 1978. "Osmotic stimulation of vasopressin release: Inhibition by tetrodotoxin." *Brain Research* 151 (2): 424–29.

Joynt, RJ. 1978. "Neuroepidemiology and the clinical neurologist." *Advances in Neurology* 19: 143–49.

Joynt, RJ, and CD Sladek. 1978. "Magnocellular neuroendocrine organization." *Transactions of the American Neurological Association* 103: 244–46.

Feibel, JH, PM Hardy, RG Campbell, MN Goldstein, and RJ Joynt. 1977. "Prognostic value of the stress response following stroke." *JAMA* 238 (13): 1374–76.

Rivera-Calimlim, L, D Tandon, F Anderson, and RJ Joynt. 1977. "The clinical picture and plasma levodopa metabolite profile of parkinsonian nonresponders. Treatment with levodopa and decarboxylase inhibitor." *Archives of Neurology* 34 (4): 228–32.

Shoulson I, D Goldblatt, M Charlton, and RJ Joynt. 1977. "Huntington's disease: Treatment with muscimol, a GABA-mimetic drug." *Transactions of the American Neurological Association* 102: 124–25.

Joynt, RJ. 1977. "Inattention syndromes in split-brain man." *Advances in Neurology* 18: 33–39.

Joynt, RL. 1976. "Dantrolene sodium: Long-term effects in patients with muscle spasticity." *Archives of Physical Medicine and Rehabilitation* 57 (5): 212–27.

Joynt, RJ, JH Feibel, and C Sladek. 1976. "Elevated antidiuretic hormone levels after cerebrovascular accidents." *Transactions of the American Neurological Association* 101: 164–68.

Feibel, JH, RG Campbell, and RJ Joynt. 1976. "Myocardial damage and cardiac arrhythmias in cerebral infarction and subarachnoid hemorrhage: Correlation with increased systemic catecholamine output." *Transactions of the American Neurological Association* 101: 242–44.

Goldstein, MN, RJ Joynt, and RB Hartley. 1975. "The long-term effects of callosal sectioning: Report of a second case." *Archives of Neurology* 32 (1): 52–53.

Iannoccone, ST, RC Griggs, WR Markesbery, and RJ Joynt. 1974. "Familial progressive external ophthalmoplegia and ragged-red fibers." *Neurology* 24 (11): 1033–38.

Joynt, RJ. 1974. "The use of bromides for epilepsy." *American Journal of Diseases of Children* 128 (3): 362–63.

Joynt, RJ. 1974 "Neurogenic paraneoplastic syndromes: The brain's uneasy peace with tumors." *Annals of the New York Academy of Sciences* 230: 342–47.

Joynt, RJ. 1973. "Phrenology in New York State." *New York State Journal of Medicine* 73 (19): 2382–84.

DeWeese, JA, CG Rob, R Satran, DO Marsh, RJ Joynt, D Summers, and C Nichols. 1973. "Results of carotid endarterectomies for transient ischemic attacks—five years later." *Annals of Surgery* 178 (3): 258–64.

Weindl, A, and RJ Joynt. 1973. "Barrier properties of the sub commissural organ." *Archives of Neurology* 29 (1): 16–22.

Scott, DE, GK Dudley, A Weindl, and RJ Joynt. 1973. "An auto radiographic analysis of hypothalamic magnocellular neurons." *Zeitschrift für Zellforschung und mikroskopische Anatomie* [Vienna, 1948] 138 (3): 421–37.

Joynt, RJ. 1973. "Neurology 1972: Chairman's address delivered before section on neurology, American Medical Association, June 21, 1972." *Neurology* 23 (2): 117–20.

Joynt, RJ. 1973. "Foam fitting faints feigning fits." *The New England Journal of Medicine* 288 (4): 219.

Weindl, A, and RJ Joynt. 1972. "Ultrastructure of the ventricular walls: Three-dimensional study of regional specialization." *Archives of Neurology* 26 (5): 420–27.

Goldstein, MN, RJ Joynt, and D Goldblatt. 1971. "Word blindness with intact central visual fields: A case report." *Neurology* 21 (9): 873–76.

Weindl, A, and RJ Joynt. 1971. "The three-dimensional appearance of regional specialization in the ventricular walls: A scanning electron microscopic study." *Transactions of the American Neurological Association* 96: 322–24.

DeWeese, JA, CG Rob, R Satran, DO Marsh, RJ Joynt, EO Lipchik, and DN Zehl. 1971. "Endarterectomy for atherosclerotic lesions of the carotid artery." *Journal of Cardiovascular Surgery* 12 (4): 299–308.

Joynt, RJ, A Weindl, and DE Scott. 1970. "Functional capacity of the deafferented supraoptic region in freely moving cats." *Neurology* 20 (4): 397.

Pribram, HF, JD Hudson, and RJ Joynt. 1969. "Posterior fossa aneurysms presenting as mass lesions." *American Journal of Roentgenology, Radium Therapy, and Nuclear Medicine* 105 (2): 334–40.

Goldstein, MN, and RJ Joynt. 1969. "Long-term follow-up of a callosal-sectioned patient: Report of a case." *Archives of Neurology* 20 (1): 96–102.

Joynt, RJ. 1968. "Foreword and general management." *Modern Treatment* 5 (6): 1211–14.

Joynt, RJ, and MN Goldstein. 1968. "Treatment of neuropathies accompanying inflammatory, vascular and neoplastic conditions." *Modern Treatment* 5 (6): 1263–71.

Calkins, RA, HF Pribram, and RJ Joynt. 1968. "Intrasellar arachnoid diverticulum: A case report." *Neurology* 18 (10): 1037–40.

Joynt, RJ, and MN Goldstein. 1968. "Twenty-seven year follow-up of callosal sectioned patient." *Transactions of the American Neurological Association* 93: 35–37.

Hudson, JD, RJ Joynt, and HF Pribram. 1967. "Water retention following neuroradiologic procedures." *Archives of Neurology* 16 (6): 624–27.

Fincham, RW, RJ Joynt, and FM Skultely. 1967. "Neurologic deficits following myelography." *Archives of Neurology* 16 (4): 410–14.

Joynt, RJ. 1966. "Verney's concept of the osmoreceptor: A review and further experimental observations." *Archives of Neurology* 14 (3): 331–44.

Joynt, RJ, and CA Cape CA. 1965. "Significance of focal delta activity in adult electroencephalogram." *Archives of Neurology* 12: 631–38.

Joynt, RJ, and GE Perret. 1965. "Familial meningiomas." *Journal of Neurology, Neurosurgery, and Psychiatry* 28: 163–64.

Joynt, RJ, G Zimmerman, and R Khalifeh. 1965. "Cerebral emboli from cardiac tumors." *Archives of Neurology* 12: 84–91.

Joynt, RJ, A Afifi, and J Harrison. 1965. "Hyponatremia in subarachnoid hemorrhage." *Archives of Neurology* 13 (6): 633–38.

Joynt, R. 1965. "Evidence in support of Verney's concept of the osmoreceptor." *Transactions of the American Neurological Association* 90: 199–202.

Afifi, A, RJ Joynt R, and J Harbison. 1965. "Inappropriate antidiuretic hormone secretion in subarachnoid hemorrhage." *Transactions of the American Neurological Association* 90: 217–18.

Green, D, RJ Joynt, and MW Vanallen. 1964. "Neuromyopathy associated with a malignant carcinoid tumor: A case report." *Archives of Internal Medicine* 114: 494–96.

Joynt, RJ, and AL Benton. 1964. "The memoir of Marc Dax on aphasia." *Neurology* 14: 851–54.

Joynt, RJ, and CA Cape. 1964. "Non-metastatic neuromuscular disorders associated with cancer." *Journal of the Iowa Medical Society* 54: 463–66.

Joynt, RJ. 1964. "Functional significance of osmosensitive units in the anterior hypothalamus." *Neurology* 14: 584–90.

Benton, AL, and RJ Joynt. 1963. "Three pioneers in the study of aphasia (Johann Schmidt, Peter Rommel, Johann A. P. Gesner)." *Journal of the History of Medicine and Allied Sciences* 18: 381–84.

Skultety, FM, and RJ Joynt. 1963. "Clinical implications of adipsia." *Journal of Neurosurgery* 20: 793–800.

Fincham, RW, AH Sahs, and RJ Joynt. 1963. "Protean manifestations of nervous system brucellosis: Case histories of a wide variety of clinical forms." *JAMA* 184: 269–75.

Joynt, RJ, and D Green. 1962. "Tonic seizures as a manifestation of multiple sclerosis." *Archives of Neurology* 6: 293–99.

Joynt, RJ, D Green, and R Green. 1962. "Musicogenic epilepsy." *JAMA* 179: 501–4.

Joynt, RJ, AL Benton, and ML Fogel. 1962. "Behavioral and pathological correlates of motor imperisistence." *Neurology* 12: 876–81.

Joynt, RJ, and AH Sahs. 1962. "Endocrine studies in pseudotumor cerebri." *Transactions of the American Neurological Association* 87: 10–13.

Barnes, CD, RJ Joynt, and BA Schottelius. 1962. "Motoneuron resting potentials in spinal shock." *The American Journal of Physiology* 203: 1113–16.

Joynt, RJ, and J Clancy. 1961. "Extreme eosinophilia during imipramine therapy." *The American Journal of Psychiatry* 118: 170–71.

Green, D, and RJ Joynt. 1961. "Auscultation of the skull in the detection of osteolytic lesions." *The New England Journal of Medicine* 264: 1203–4.

Joynt, RJ, and GE Perret. 1961. "Meningiomas in a mother and daughter: Cases without evidence of neurofibromatosis." *Neurology* 11: 164–65.

Joynt, RJ. 1961. "Centenary of patient 'Tan': His contribution to the problem of aphasia." *Archives of Internal Medicine* 108: 953–56.

Benton, AL, and RJ Joynt. 1960. "Early descriptions of aphasia." *Archives of Neurology* 3: 205–22.

Bell, WE, RJ Joynt, and AH Sahs. 1960. "Low spinal fluid pressure syndromes." *Neurology* 10: 512–21.

Green, D, and RJ Joynt. 1959. "Vascular accidents to the brain stem associated with neck manipulation." *Journal of the American Medical Association* 170 (5): 522–24.

Joynt, RJ. 1959. "An EEG artefact in palatal myoclonus." *Electroencephalogram.* Clin. Neurophysiology Suppl. 11 (1): 158–60.

Benton, AL, and RJ Joynt. 1959. "Reaction time in unilateral cerebral disease." *Confinia Neurologica* 19 (3): 247–56.

Joynt, RJ. 1958. "Micro-electrode studies of cerebellar electrical activity in the frog." *Journal of Physiology* 144 (1): 23–37.

Joynt, RJ. 1958. "Mechanism of production of papilledema in the Guillain-Barre syndrome." *Neurology* 8 (1): 8–12.

Joynt, RJ, and AH Sahs. 1956. "Brain swelling of unknown cause." *Neurology* 6 (11): 801–3.

Kaelber, WW, and RJ Joynt. 1956. "Tremor production in cats given chlorpromazine." *Proceedings of the Society for Experimental Biology and Medicine* 92 (2): 399–402.

Books and Chapters

Joynt, RJ, et al. "Report of the Working Group on Disability in U.S. Presidents." In *Managing Crisis: Presidential Disability and The Twenty-Fifth Amendment*, edited by RE Gilbert. New York: Fordham University Press, 2000.

Joynt, RJ, WL Adams, RD Adelman, CA Alessi, and N Alexander. "Aging and the Nervous System." In *The Merck Manual of Geriatrics*, edited by MH Beers and R Berkow. Whitehouse Station, NJ: Merck Research Laboratories, Division of Merck & Co., Inc., 2000.

Stein, JH, LA Goldsmith, RJ Joynt, J Cohen, GA Kimmich, VG Laties, RE Marquis, GB Forbes, PL LaCelle, JF Sollenberger, LW McClure, C Hollihan, RA Lawrence, HJ Kitzman, BA Powers, MH Schmitt, RJ Billings, JW Bartlett, and N Bolger. *The University of Rochester Medical Center: Teaching, Discovering, Caring*. Edited by J Cohen and RJ Joynt. Rochester, NY: University of Rochester Press, 2000.

Goodman, AD, LM Alderson, CG Benesch, MJ Berg, T Braun, P Calabresi, RJ Joynt, D Mock, SR Schwid, LS Williams, and JP Wymer. "Current Therapy." In *Clinical Neurology*, edited by RJ Joynt and RC Griggs. Philadelphia, PA: Lippincott-Raven Publishers, 1998.

Goodman, AD, CG Benesch, M Berg, T Braun, P Calabresi, R Holloway, RJ Joynt, O Samuels, LS Williams, and J Wymer. "Current Therapy." In *Clinical Neurology*, edited by RJ Joynt and RC Griggs. Philadelphia, PA: Lippincott-Raven Publishers, 1996.

Jozefowicz, RF, CG Benesch, M Berg, P Calabresi, T Dimitsopulos, A Goodman, R Holloway, RJ Joynt, LS Williams, and J Wojcieszek. "Current Therapy." In *Clinical Neurology*, edited by RJ Joynt. Philadelphia, PA: Lippincott-Raven Publishers, 1995.

Joynt, RJ. "Normal Aging and Patterns of Neurologic Disease." In *The Merck Manual of Geriatrics*, edited by WB Abrams and R Berkow. Rahway, NJ: Merck Sharp & Dohme Research Laboratories, 1995.

Joynt, RJ, and J Greenlaw. "The Informed Consent: Consensus Conference Guidelines for Drug Trials in Memory Disorders." In *The Aging Series*, edited by N Canal, V Hachinski, G McKhann, M Franceschi M. New York: Raven Press, 1993.

McNeill, TH, and RJ Joynt. "Ependymal." In *Diseases of the Nervous System*, edited by AK Asbury, GM McKhann, and WI McDonald. Philadelphia, PA: WB Saunders Company, 1992.

Joynt, RJ (Consulting Editor). *Textbook of Adolescent Medicine*. Edited by G Commerci, R Kreipe, E McAnarney, and D Orr. Philadelphia, PA: WB Saunders Company, 1992.

Joynt, RJ. "Neurologic Disorders." In *The Merck Manual of Geriatrics*, edited by WB Abrams and R Berkow. Rahway, NJ: Merck Sharp & Dohme Research Laboratories, 1990.

Joynt, RJ. "Hughlings Jackson and American Neurology." In *Hierarchies in Neurology*, edited by C Kennard and M Swash. New York: Springer-Verlag, 1989.

Joynt, RJ. "Neurology." In *Medical and Health Annual*, edited by E Bernstein. Chicago, IL: Encyclopedia Britannica, Inc., 1989.

Joynt, RJ, ed. *Clinical Neurology*. 4 vols. Philadelphia, PA: Lippincott Raven. 1988.

Joynt, RJ. "Neurology." In *Medical and Health Annual*, edited by Ellen Bernstein. Chicago, IL: Encyclopedia Britannica, Inc., 1988.

Joynt, RJ, and T McNeill. "Ependymal." In *Diseases of the Nervous System*, edited by AK Asbury, GM McKhann, WI McDonald. Philadelphia, PA: WB Saunders Company, 1986.

Joynt, RJ, and I Shoulson. "Dementia." In *Clinical Neuropsychology*, edited by KM Heilman and E Valenstein. New York: Oxford University Press, 1985.

Joynt, RJ. "Alzheimer's Disease." In *Conn's Current Therapy*, edited by RE Rakel. Philadelphia, PA: WB Saunders Company, 1985.

Joynt, RJ, G Honch, A Rubin, and R Trudell. "Disorders of the Occipital Lobe." In *Handbook of Neurology*, edited by PJ Vinken, GW Bruyn, and HL Klawans. UK: Elsevier Science Publishers, 1985.

Gas, DM, MFD Notter, LB Dick, AL Kraus, SH Okawara, SW Wechkin, and RJ Joynt. "Cholinergic Neurons Transplanted into the Neocortex and Hippocampus of Primates: Studies on African Green Monkeys." In *Neural Grafting in the Mammalian CNS*, edited by A Bjorklund and U Stenevi. United Kingdom: Elsevier Science Publishers, 1985.

Joynt, RJ. "Laboratory Procedures." In *Merck Manual*, edited by R Berkow. Rahway, NJ: Merck Sharp & Dohme Research Laboratories, Division of Merck & Co., Inc., 1983.

Joynt, RJ. "Neurological Examination." In *Merck Manual*, edited by R Berkow. Rahway, NJ: Merck Sharp & Dohme Research Laboratories, Division of Merck & Co., Inc., 1983.

Sahs, AH, and RJ Joynt. "Meningitis." In *Baker's Clinical Neurology*, edited by AB Baker. Philadelphia, PA: Lippincott Williams and Wilkins, 1979.

NOTES

Chapter One

1. Mary Ellen Joynt Thoman, Patricia ("Patty") Joynt Olson, and Margaret ("Peggy") Joynt Bushwaller.

2. According to local legend, the name "Le Mars" is made up of the first initials of the town's first women settlers: Lucy Underhill, Elizabeth Parson, Mary Weare, Anna Blair, Rebecca Smith, and Sarah Reynolds.

3. Based on Joynt family reminiscences, as reinforced by Arthur Schlesinger, Jr., in *The Coming of the New Deal, 1933–35* (New York: Houghton Mifflin).

4. Bob, whose appetite for unusual words was enormous, must have loved this one: "something outstanding; a decisive blow that settles a matter" (*Webster's*, 11th ed.).

5. Thomas E. Starzl, *The Puzzle People: Memoirs of a Transplant Surgeon* (Pittsburgh, PA: University of Pittsburgh Press, 1992), 22.

Chapter Two

1. Perhaps the beginning of this American Irishman's Anglophilia.

2. Nor was Wavell supported by Winston Churchill, an opponent of independence for India.

Chapter Six

1. A. Benton, *Exploring the History of Neuropsychology* (New York: Oxford University Press), vii.

Chapter Seven

1. R. J. Joynt, "The Urge to Grow and the Urge to Stay Small: The Dilemma of the Post-War Years," in *To Each His Farthest Star: University of Rochester Medical Center, 1925–1975*, ed. J. Romano and J. Cohen (Rochester, NY: University of Rochester Press, 1975), 364.

2. Five years later, Molinari would be called to Washington to head the Stroke Section at the National Institute for Neurological and Communicative Disorders and Stroke.

Chapter Eight

1. A neurological test to determine the reaction of the big toe when the sole of the foot is stimulated.

Chapter Nine

1. "Pogo" was the title and central character of a long-running comic strip by the cartoonist Walt Kelly, popular during the 1950s to 1960s.

2. Update by substituting the word "computer" or "smart phone" for telephone.

3. Popular author and arbiter of good manners.

Chapter Twelve

1. James F. Toole and Robert J. Joynt, eds., *Presidential Disability: Papers, Discussions, and Recommendations on the Twenty-Fifth Amendment and Issues of Inability and Disability in Presidents of the United States* (Rochester, NY: University of Rochester Press, 2001), 124–25.

Chapter Thirteen

1. The street had another literary reference in the 1930 play (and later film) *The Barretts of Wimpole Street*, based on the romance between the poet Robert Browning and Elizabeth Barrett.

Chapter Fifteen

1. Previously it had been a double position, Vice President and Dean of the Schools of Medicine and Dentistry.

2. Overseen by the nonprofit Rochester Area Hospital Corporation (RAHC). Dr. Bob served a term as president of RAHC during the early '90s.

3. Also the author of this remembrance.

4. Later chancellor at UCSF and eventually dean of Harvard's medical school.

5. A *Festschrift* is a collection of writings published in honor of a scholar, usually presented during his or her lifetime. In this case the "writings" consist of transcripts of the scientific papers presented at the *Festschrift*.

Chapter Sixteen

1. Creatine phosphokinase (CPK) test, which measures the amount of CPK in the blood. High levels usually indicate stress or injury to the heart or other muscles.

2. In 2005, playing in the annual Robert Joynt Golf Classic with neurology residents, his long pitch to the green landed in the hole. "Now, that's how it should be done!" he exclaimed.

Chapter Seventeen

1. Previously the longest-running nonmusical play on Broadway.

2. Professor of physics at the University of Wisconsin. Called "Tup" by his father, a name coined at the boy's birth in Cambridge: "Why, he's no bigger than a thruppence!"

3. An executive vice president of the Arnold World Wide Advertising Agency in Boston.

4. President of Joynt Packaging International in Victor, New York.

5. Mrs. Michael Pieper, Pittsford, New York. Managing editor of *Neurology*.

6. Mrs. Edmund Wodarksi, Pittsford, New York. A psychometrist at the University of Rochester Medical Center.

7. Mrs. Donald Goodman, Pittsford, New York. Retired from the M. K. Gandhi Institute for Nonviolence at the University of Rochester and substitute art teacher at a local high school.

8. In graduate school, Bob once fought the Russian chess champion Anatoly Karpov to a draw.

9. Formally and fondly known as the La Trappe Creek Historical and Ecological Society International.

Chapter Eighteen

1. In the folder he was carrying was the unfinished draft of his last Sherlock Holmes mystery.

In this stirring collection of essays, author Nancy Bolger leads the reader through the extraordinary life of Robert J. Joynt, MD, PhD, one of the most influential neurologists of the last half century. The story begins on the small-town streets of Iowa and takes us through military service and medical school, down the wedding aisle, and ultimately to a long and successful career at the University of Rochester, where Dr. Joynt became the first chair of the newly created Department of Neurology in 1966. Along the way, we accompany Dr. Joynt on his travels to India, Canada, Ireland, London and Cambridge in England, and many other places, including a much-loved lakeside retreat in Minnesota where the family vacationed year after year. These pages tell of not only Dr. Joynt's life but also of those who inspired him, and how he in turn became a remarkable inspiration to others.

Nancy W. Bolger is a writer and editor for the University of Rochester Medical Center. In 1992 she received the Robert G. Fenley Award of Distinction for Medical Science Writing from the Association of American Medical Colleges.